LAND REFORMS AND SOCIAL JUSTICE IN INDIA

LAND REFORMS AND SOCIAL JUSTICE IN INDIA

Dr. N. Kannan

ABHIJEET PUBLICATIONS
DELHI 110094

ABHIJEET PUBLICATIONS
2/46 Tukhmeerpur Extension
Delhi-110 094
Phone: 011-22960492, 65698474
E-mail: abhijeetpublication@gmail.com

LAND REFORMS AND SOCIAL JUSTICE IN INDIA

First Published 2008

ISBN 978-81-89886-80-6

PRINTED IN INDIA

Published by J.K. Singh for Abhijeet Publications, Delhi-110 094, Lasertypeset by Gaurav Graphics, New Delhi and Printed at Himanshu Printers, Delhi.

Dedicated

to

My Parents

Mr. M. NATARAJAN

& N. MALLIKA

Preface

Institutional changes in India is the need of the hour today. Since the land holding pattern in India is largely found in hierarchical manner. The distribution of land holding both in rural and urban areas is largely found in an exorbitant manner. The government has enacted various legislative measures and ceiling on land holdings for the purpose of fair distribution of land. Hence tenurial system, land to the tiller of soil, and other stern measures form the serious threat to the original landlords. Since from independence zamindari system and the outdated Fazali Act which hinders the distribution of land in an equal manner in all the states.

First generation land reforms like Zamindari Abolition Act, etc. have helped certain backward castes in UP and Bihar to come to the fore and have a grip on political system of the state. Success of Operation Barga in West Bengal has helped share croppers and landless labourers to have a stake in the land and improved their economic lot. Similarly other land reforms in other states have helped certain groups. But taking land reforms on an all India basis, and giving benefits of land reforms to Scheduled

Castes, Scheduled Tribes, most backward sections of the society, and even giving proprietory rights of land to women is the crying need of the hour. This book covers all these aspects in a lucid and simple manner. It answers to questions like why land reforms are necessary and in what manner it should be done.

I take this opportunity to express my heart felt thanks to our respected College Secretary, Shri K. Raghunathan, B.Com., B.L., Advocate for his immense help.

My heartfelt thanks to our respected principal Dr. K. Anbarasu M.Sc., M. Phil., P.h.D., who is the source of inspiration in writing this book. I owe my affectionate thanks to respected Professor and HOD of Economics Sri S.X. Prabhu for his enthustitic help

I will be failing in myduty if I don't express my thanks to former Prof. and HOD of Economics Dr. P.S. Mohan and other learned Professors and well wishers for their timely help. Again I place my sincere thanks to my parents Mr. M. Natarajan and Mrs. N. Mallika for their financial support. Lastly I solemnly place my heartfelt thanks to Sri. J.K. Singh, Abhijeet Publications, Delhi.

Suggestions for improvement are always welcome.

DR. N. KANNAN

TIRUCHIRAPPALLI

JUNE 2008

Contents

1

Land Reforms in India Since 1947: Achievements and Failures

There is no doubt that land reforms are an essential condition for promoting agricultural development and for initiating the changes in agrarian society that are required for its rapid transformation. This has been demonstrated by the experience of several countries in East Asia, particularly of Japan. It was clearly recognized in India also from the beginning of planned development in the early 1950s. However, despite this recognition, the progress made over the last four decades and a-half has been insignificant—except in the northern and eastern regions of the country, where extensive areas were under a system of revenue farming through intermediaries (known as zamindars) during the period of British rule, and in a few States such as Kerala and West Bengal over the last two or three decades.

Zamindari System

Where revenue farming prevailed, in continuation of a system that the British inherited from the earlier Mughal rule, there were intermediaries (i.e. zamindars) to whom was contracted the collection of land revenue. For some years towards the close of the 18th century, the East India Company made direct collections with the objective of exacting as much revenue as possible from land. But, soon after, it was decided to make settlements by auction to the highest bidders for a period of five years, and then to a system of annual settlement with zamindars—which proved to be no better. Following a decennial settlement towards the close of the 1780s, it was declared permanent in 1793. This was, however, a very severe land tax, ruining millions of actual cultivators and producing disastrous social, economic and political consequences. Though the rights of tenants were never intended to be forgotten, no effective step was taken to regulate rent and protect the rights of tenants. The system of permanent settlement with zamindars was nevertheless extended to cover the provinces of Bengal, Bihar, East Uttar Pradesh, North Madras and parts of Assam and Orissa; the intermediaries were not always known as zamindars, sometimes being named as *taluqdars* (as in Uttar Pradesh) or *malguzars*. (as in the Central Provinces).

Despite various improvements and relief measures adopted during the subsequent period of British rule, there was—at the time India gained political Independence—a complex layering of rights over land, from those of the State as superior landlord (or ultimate owner) down through those of the sub-landlords and several tiers of tenants. As Daniel Thorner observed in a series of lectures delivered in 1955 at the Delhi School of Economics, "the maintenance of this hierarchical structure of interest in land has required, in effect, that quite a substantial proportion of the produce be reserved for persons who perform no agricultural labour". Consequently, "the working Kisan was left with no surplus to invest in better implements, improved seed or fertilizer, and in any case no real incentive to increase his productivity; (and) for the landless mazdoor, there was even less point in any attempt to raise his efficiency". Thorner described the entire complex of relations as a multi-faceted and built-in "depressor", which was the root cause of the stagnation in Indian agriculture and much of the social and economic injustices that prevailed in the rural society.

Abolition of Intermediary Interests: In 1947, the zamindari system covered nearly three-fifths of the total area of private land-holdings in nine provinces of British India, the *mahalwari* system about five per cent, and the *raiyatwari* system (under which the government was the sole landlord) the remaining one-third. Among the measures of land reform introduced thereafter, the first and foremost was the abolition of intermediary interests in land—intermediary interests connoting the hierarchy of proprietory interests that existed between the State and the actual occupier of the land. As briefly described earlier, these interests constituted one or more layers of various amorphous and parasitic groups that appropriated a substantial share of the produce of the land and harassed the cultivators in diverse ways. The term "intermediary" would include zamindars as well as all kinds of tenure-holders.

Attempting a broad assessment of the measures taken and implemented for the abolition of zamindari tenures, Wolf Ladejinsky—well-known the world over for his active role in the land reforms undertaken in Japan when under the occupation of United States after the Second World War— observed as follows:

"Despite opposition and administrative and technical problems, the Zamindary tenures were virtually abolished. Not all have benefitted equally and not all the 20 million cultivators affected have received permanent, heritable, and transferable rights. Nevertheless the effort was a great step toward a reconstruction of Indian agriculture. The measures because it was politically popular to abolish an agricultural system full of abuses imposed by a foreign power. With the British gone the government went about drafting the necessary legislation, the zamindars were abolished despite the opposition of the landlords, lack of financial means and insufficient administrative and technical staff. Not every 't' was crossed and every 'i' was dotted, but the job was done". [Cf. Wolf Ladejinsky, *Agrarian Reform As Unfinished Business,* Oxford University Press, 1977, p. 362].

The estimate of 20 million tenants brought into direct relationship with the State is perhaps a little too low. According to the Uttar Pradesh Zamindari Abolition Committee Report, Uttar Pradesh alone had about 14 million superior tenants with recorded rights and, according to the Report of the Revenue Commission in Bengal, it had over six million *raiyati* interests even after making allowance for the large-scale evictions that took place. A more recent estimate places the number of erstwhile tenants brought into direct relationship with the State at about 25 million [Cf. P.S. Appu, Land Reforms in India—A Survey of Policy, Legislation and Implementation (mimeograph), Land Reforms Unit, Lal Bahadur Shastri National Academy of Administration, Mussoorie, 1995].

Shift in the Balance of Power

A report of the Task Force on Agrarian Relations appointed by the Planning Commission in the early 1970s has observed that, with the abolition of intermediary interests, ownership of land became more broad-based and the erstwhile tenants acquired a higher social status (though, as a result of the tenancy laws in the decades prior to Independence, the superior tenants had already been enjoying security of tenure and fixity of rent). In the decades that followed, political power also shifted to these classes. "The most visible demonstration of this shift in political power is the substantial presence of persons belonging to the upper layers of the so-called backward castes in the leadership of the political parties. In the last two decades, members of the backward castes even became Chief Ministers in Uttar Pradesh and Bihar. Such a development was inconceivable in the pre-reform era. Undoubtedly, the abolition of intermediary interests paved the way for a remarkable shift in the balance of power" (*Ibid.*, P.S. Appu).

Shortcomings: There were, of course, also some unwelcome consequences and shortcomings like most important of which was that the reform led to large-scale ejectment of peasants from the land they had been cultivating for generations. Those who suffered most from such ejectment were tenants-at-will and share-croppers. The reform afforded offered no protection to vast numbers of them. As Daniel Thorner had earlier observed, the laws of Manu and the socio-religious pretensions of the higher castes did not require that supervision of agricultural operations be done by owners in person or on the spot. Evictions reduced the status of many, from that of tenant to that of share-cropper and agricultural labourer. The bottom layer of the peasantry thus received no benefit from reform, and naturally the reform failed to achieve of the proclaimed goal of "land to the tiller" (*Ibid.*, P.S. Appu).

Security of Tenure: With the abolition of most of the intermediary interests the whole country came under more or less the same kind of tenurial system. However, even though the *raiyatwari* system was supposed to have been one of peasant proprietorship, leasing out of land was in practice widespread in the raiyatwari areas also. In the erstwhile zamindari areas too there had been subleasing. The greater part of all such leases were oral and terminable at will. Several measures were, therefore, adopted after Independence to afford security of tenure and fixity of rent to the erstwhile under-tenants in zamindari areas and tenants in *raiyatwari* areas.

Five Year Plans and Tenancy Reforms

The, important guidelines laid down in the Five Year Plans for the reform of tenancy were the following: first, that the rent should not exceed the level of one-fifth to one-fourth of the gross produce: secondly, the tenants should be accorded permanent rights in the lands they cultivated subject to a limited right of resumption to be granted to the landowners; and thirdly, that in respect of non-resumable lands, the landlord-tenant relationship should be ended by conferring ownership rights on the tenants.

Fair rents have been fixed within the limits prescribed in the Five Year Plans in all States except those of the Punjab, Haryana and the Andhra area of Andhra Pradesh; even in the case of the three States mentioned above, the legally fixed fair rent is only marginally higher than the level indicated in the Plans. The second objective of giving security of tenure to tenants has not however, been attained in most States. The legal protection extended to tenants proved to be ineffective because of the shortcomings in the laws and the generally poor implementation of the enacted laws. As for protection of ownership rights or conferment of such rights, only about 11 million tenants operating no more than four per cent of the total operated area in the country benefited from such action; and most of these beneficiaries were confined to the seven States of Assam, Gujarat, Himachal Pradesh, Karnataka, Kerala, Maharashtra and West Bengal, leaving the tenants in the other States with practically no benefits.

West Bengal and Kerala Stand Out

Even in the seven States mentioned above, tenancy reform led to large-scale eviction of tenants. Share-croppers remained by and large beyond the pale of tenancy reform everywhere except in West Bengal over the 1980s. And only in West Bengal and Kerala were the lowest rungs of peasant society benefited by the implementation of tenancy reform. In West Bengal, the rights of about 14 lakh sharecroppers have been protected, and in Kerala nearly three lakh rural poor (mostly agricultural labourers) have become owners of tiny homesteads of one-tenth acre each. In Kerala, as a result of the reform and the more recent migration of labour to West Asia, agricultural labourers have been able to use their power derived from trade unionism to raise their daily wage rates to about the same level as in Punjab and Haryana from the 1980s.

Tenancy in New Form: The area under tenancy in the country as a whole has, in consequence of all the measures mentioned above, declined from over one-half of the total operated area to about 15 per cent of the total area now. However, tenancy reform has not brought to an end the system of absentee ownership of land nor led to disappearance of tenancies. Tenancies have instead been pushed underground and most of the tenancies that still exist take the form of informal crop-sharing arrangements.

Ceilings on Holdings

One facet of land reforms that was advocated by the Planning Commission without much conviction was the imposition of ceilings on agricultural holdings. Apart from the commercial plantations of tree crops concentrated in a few areas there were few large farms in India like those in Europe and America. The typical large holding in the country was but an assortment of scattered pieces of land bereft of fixed assets spread over one or more villages. Where the owner of such a large holding was an absentee landlord he got the land cultivated through tenants-at-will. Imposition of ceilings would have certainly resulted in part of such land getting passed on to the ownership of those who had been cultivating it, and the result would have been fuller utilization of land and labour leading to enhanced output. There also existed adequate economic and social justification for the imposition of ceilings and the redistribution of surplus land. These were essentially the reasons why the Planning Commission advocated the measures.

Lack of Political Will

However, the enactment of the ceiling laws was preceded by a protracted debate spread over several years. This gave plenty of time to enable landowners to dispose of the land that would have been declared surplus. Moreover, since the guidelines given by the Planning Commission were flexible and the details were left to be determined by the States, there was great diversity in respect of the ceiling actually imposed by them, classification of land on the basis of which ceilings were determined, unit of application, and allowance for the size of the family, exemption to special categories of owners, treatment of transfers and partitions, and the quantum of compensation. Consequently, the implementation of ceiling legislation was poor and, by 1970, only about one million hectares of surplus land had been vested in government and only about one-half of that could be distributed. There is, of course, no doubt that the most important reason for the dismal performance was the total lack of political will.

Efforts by Centre and States

The programmes adopted in pursuance of the above policy ere the abolition of intermediary interests, tenancy reform, n of ceilings on agricultural holdings and consolidation of holdings. During the last 50 years, the Central and State governments devoted a great deal of effort to the delineation and refinement of policy, the enactment and amendment of the laws and their implementation. The enacted laws have been implemented at differing levels of competence or incompetence. Broadly stated, the implementation of the laws for the abolition of intermediary interests was far more satisfactory than the implementation of the laws enacted in later years for the reform of tenancy and the imposition of ceilings.

Abolition of Intermediaries: As a result of the abolition of intermediary interests, some 2.5 crore erstwhile superior tenants became landowners holding land directly under the government. They were freed from the illegal exactions of the zamindars. The erstwhile principal tenants acquired a higher social and political status leading to a shift in the rural power structure. Large areas of privately owned forests and wasteland vested in the State. Though the beneficial results were substantial, the reforms led to some unwelcome consequences. The most important evil effect was that it led to the large-scale ejectment of poor peasants from the land they had been cultivating for generations. That happened because the law permitted the intermediaries to retain their home farms, no limit was put on the area of land they could retain, the term 'personal cultivation' was loosely defined and no protection was given to share-croppers and other tenants-at-will. The reform would have yielded far better results if steps had been taken simultaneously to limit the size of the home farms and give protection to the tenants-at-will on those farms.

Tenancy Pushed Underground: Regarding tenancy reform, three important guidelines were laid down in the Five Year Plans. First, rent should not exceed one-fifth to one-fourth of the gross produce: second, the tenants should be accorded permanent rights in the lands they cultivated subject to a limited right of resumption to be granted to the landowners; and third, in respect of non-resumable land the landlord-tenant relationship should be ended by conferring ownership rights on tenants. While formulating the policy the overriding consideration was that the measures adopted for the protection of tenants should not seriously affect the landowners. Considering the character of the political power-structure and the fact that the owners who had let out their lands were numerous and that they had considerable political clout, the adoption of such a pro-landlord policy was inevitable. In order to protect the interests of the landowners every tenancy law contained a provision for the resumption of a part of the tenanted land by the landowners for 'personal cultivation'.

In all the laws, the term 'personal cultivation' was loosely defined so as to include cultivation of land without putting in one's own labour or even personal supervision. The laws also permitted the voluntary surrender of tenancies. The inevitable consequence was the surrender of numerous tenancies under duress though shown on paper as voluntary surrenders. Most of the tenancies in the Raiyatwari areas and under-tenancies in the Zamindari areas were oral and informal share-cropping arrangements. They were seldom entered in the land records. Some laws deliberately left the share-croppers out of the purview of the tenancy law. Even in States where the law recognised the share-croppers as tenants, they could hardly avail themselves of the benefit purported to be conferred by the law as it was extremely difficult to prove the existence of tenancy. When all efforts to mend tenancy failed, it was decided that tenancies should be ended. The new policy was that the leasing out of land should be prohibited and all tenants should be made owners of the land they had been cultivating, on payment of compensation. The shift in policy did not, however, yield better results. For the problem of proving the existence of tenancies continued. The main consequence of the new policy was to push tenancies underground.

Repercussions: What did our efforts spread over half-a-century to reform tenancy achieve? It has been estimated that at Independence over one half of the operated area was under tenancy. As a result of tenancy reform, tenants acquired ownership rights in about four per cent of the operated area in the country. The seven States of Assam. Gujarat, Himachal Pradesh, Karnataka, Kerala, Maharashtra and West Bengal account for 97 per cent of the beneficiaries. The superior tenants who became owners on the abolition of intermediaries are left out in this computation. In the case of West Bengal the *bargadars* whose rights were protected, but did not acquire ownership rights, have been taken into account. Everywhere the immediate consequence of tenancy reform was the large-scale ejectment of tenants

Sharecroppers derived little benefit from the programme except in West Bengal. Tenancy reform has led to a sharp fall in the area of land under tenancy. From over one half of the operated area at the time of Independence, tenancy, mostly concealed, has come down to about 15 per cent. The rural poor have lost access to about 30 per cent of the operated area as a result of tenancy reform. If tenancies are allowed legally, tenants can acquire rights in the land they cultivate and the rural poor will have access to a larger area of agricultural land. In many States, tenancy reform has also resulted in landowners leaving their land uncultivated. For, they fear that they may lose the land if they lease it out. The lifting of the ban on leasing may encourage such landowners to lease out their land. The result will be better utilization of the available land, fuller absorption of human labour and increased farm output.

Ceiling laws: To reduce the disparities in the ownership of land and make some land available for distribution to the landless agricultural labourers and poor peasants with tiny holdings, the Second Five Year Plan recommended the imposition of ceilings on agricultural holdings. In accordance with that recommendation, by 1961 all States enacted ceiling laws. The Planning Commission had given only broad guidelines with considerable flexibility. The inevitable consequence was wide variations between the laws of different States in the matter of the level of ceiling, unit of application, exemptions, etc. The enactment of the ceiling laws was preceded by a public debate. Naturally, all alert landowners took steps in good time to distribute the surplus land among their relations, friends and dependents, and in some cases they made paper transactions showing transfer to fictitious trusts. Because of the ambivalence in the formulation of policy, the shortcomings and loopholes in the laws and inefficient implementation, the ceiling laws did not yield any worthwhile results. By the late sixties it had become clear that the ceiling laws would not achieve anything. Yet, in the context of the radical stance adopted by the then ruling party, land reforms in general, and ceilings in particular, received a great deal of attention in the late sixties and early seventies. After protracted deliberations, revised guidelines were issued in July 1972. The revised guidelines brought down the levels of ceiling, insisted upon the family being made the unit of application and did away with most exemptions. There was, however, no improvement in the quality of implementation. As a result of the implementation of the old and the revised laws, only less than two per cent of the agricultural land could be redistributed. The reasons for the poor performance were flaws in the policy, the built-in loopholes in the laws, absence of political will, frequent judicial interventions, administrative inadequacies and lack of organization on the part of the potential beneficiaries.

Consolidation & Farm Growth: Consolidation of holdings has been completed in Punjab, Haryana and Uttar Pradesh. The programme has not. however, made any headway in the other States. Consolidation of holdings played a significant role in facilitating fast agricultural growth in Punjab, Haryana and Western Uttar Pradesh.

To sum up, the programmes of land reform implemented since Independence did not lead to any significant redistribution of land, or, the removal of all the obstacles to increasing agricultural productivity. The laws for the abolition of intermediary interests were implemented fairly well, but in the case of tenancy reform and ceilings on holdings, the policies adopted were ambivalent and there were large gaps between policy and legislation and between legislation and implementation. We have seen that these two programmes taken together led to the redistribution of only about six per cent of the operated area. That was insignificant compared to the redistributive effect of the land reforms implemented in Japan, the People's Republic of China, South Korea, Taiwan and Vietnam. The Indian land reform did not lead to any significant redistribution of land, nor did it succeed in removing some of the persisting obstacles to raising agricultural productivity. Yet, it will be a mistake to write it off as a non-event. It did bring about great changes. It did not make the actual tiller the owner of his land in all cases. But it did away with the numerous layers of parasitic intermediaries between the State and the cultivator. The Zamindari system with all its notorious abuses has disappeared yielding place to a new rural power structure in which the erstwhile landlords share power with their former substantial tenants. The balance of political power has shifted considerably. The reforms, however, left untouched the bottom layer of the agrarian structure consisting of agricultural labourers, share-croppers and rural artisans. They received little benefit from the reforms.

Post-Reform Scenario

When India become independent, agriculture had been stagnating for several decades at low levels of productivity. The prevailing pattern of rights in the land and sharing of the produce stood in the way of the adoption of modern farming practices and the application of optimum doses of labour, capital and other inputs. The period since the mid-sixties has witnessed a sea change in the situation. Indian agriculture is no longer stagnant. In fact, it has shown considerable dynamism during the last three decades. In the context of chronic food shortages and rising imports a new agricultural strategy was adopted in the mid-sixties. The essence of that strategy was to concentrate all efforts in selected districts with potential for rapid growth. The introduction of the new strategy coincided with the emergence of high yielding varieties of wheat seeds. Taking into account the great potential of the new seeds the strategy was modified laying emphasis on the introduction of those seeds and multiple cropping. The great spurt in food production that followed was hailed as the Green Revolution. The increase in food production was impressive by any standard. In the first phase of the Green Revolution, the spectacular growth in output was largely confined to one cereal—wheat, and one compact area—the western half of the Gangetic valley. There was a marked resistance to the spread of the Green Revolution to the equally well-endowed Eastern half of the Gangetic valley. The second phase of the Green Revolution witnessed marked increase in the output of rice and the spread of the Green Revolution to other well-endowed areas. There has been remarkable growth in output in the Eastern half of the Gangetic valley also, but the full potential is yet to be realized. The spectre of famine has vanished and a large buffer stock of food grains has been built up. There is, however, a dark side to this rosy picture. Because of the failure of land reforms and other programmes for the redistribution of assets, and the inadequate growth of employment, widespread poverty and unsatisfied hunger coexist with mounting stocks of food grains. Another unwelcome aspect of the so-called Green Revolution is the widening gap between the large farmers and the small holders and between regions. Though a number of such problems still remain, the agrarian scene today is totally different from what it was at Independence. It is high time that we took a fresh look at our land policy bearing in mind the great changes that have taken place during the last three decades.

It is not only the agrarian situation that has changed. Significant changes have taken place in the political, social and economic fields. If political will in favour of purposeful land reform was weak at Independence and weaker still later on, it is non-existent today. Land reform has gone out of the agenda of political parties. This was perhaps inevitable in the context of the great changes that have taken place in the social and economic fields. With the abolition of intermediary interests, the erstwhile superior tenants belonging mostly to the upper and middle castes acquired a higher social status. Rise in agricultural productivity, higher incomes from cultivation and steep rise in land values have greatly augmented their economic strength. Substantial landowners who wield great authority in rural India are bitterly opposed to ceilings on agricultural holdings. They are able to have their way because no serious efforts have been made to organize the poor peasants in favour of progressive reforms. As far as tenancy is concerned, there is a certain commonality of interest between all landowners, whether they be large, small or even marginal. They are all passionately attached to their land and all of them are opposed to conferring benefits on insecure tenants. In the first round of land reform, only the intermediaries were adversely affected. They were few in number and were weak politically. They had also become unpopular by aligning themselves with the colonial power. So it was easy enough to abolish intermediary interests. And it was done without hurting them much. But injuring the interests of the present class of landowners is a different proposition. They are numerous, they have become prosperous and they have considerable political clout. At the time of Independence, they did not wield much political and economic power, and so with a modicum of political will the reforms could have been implemented. But now that the landowners have waxed strong, no political party would like to incur their wrath. The most opportune moment for progressive reforms passed long ago.

Revamping the Policy: Different Views

There are also serious doubts about the wisdom of persisting with the old package of land policies. Though there is general agreement on the need to revise the land policy, there are sharp differences about the lines on which the policy should be recast. One school believes that the agrarian constraints no longer exist in the old form, and that-even if they exist in some pockets, they can be overcome by the adoption of modern technology and necessary institutional support for the supply of credit and other inputs. They argue that the ceiling laws should be abrogated and that all restrictions on the leasing of agricultural land should be removed. The second school also believes that there is the need to revise the land policy in the context of the changes that have taken place during the last four decades, but it will be unwise to abrogate the ceiling laws. The existing ceiling laws should be enforced' and the surplus land should be distributed. No useful purpose will be served by scaling down the ceilings. As far as tenancy is concerned, this school is in favour of removing the restrictions on the leasing out of land and allowing clandestine tenancies to come to the surface. The third point of view is that despite all the changes that have taken place, it will not be possible to promote sustained agricultural growth commensurate with social and economic justice unless some minimal institutional reforms are carried out. Admittedly, the opportune moment for purposeful land reform passed long ago. It is also true that the technological breakthrough and the so-called Green Revolution have rendered the needed institutional reforms even more difficult. But instead of rendering land reform irrelevant, the adoption of new technology has, as a matter of fact, highlighted the urgent need for institutional changes.

While I am in complete agreement with the view that some measures of land reform are urgently needed for fostering agricultural growth, particularly in the eastern half of the Gangetic valley and some other well-endowed areas, I am not optimistic about the emergence of a climate favourable to land reform in the immediate future. In the present context, a constituency in favour of purposeful land reform can be created only by engineering a coalition to promote the self-interest of political parties, the captains of industry and the rural poor. As of now, such a development is only a theoretical possibility.

After having closely observed the formulation of land policy, the enactment of land reform laws and their implementation during the last 25 years, I have come to the conclusion that it is high time that we made some substantial changes in our land policy. My suggestions are given below.

Tenancy Reform

The restrictions on the leasing out of land have only led to tenancies being pushed underground. As long as a class of landowners who shun physical labour and a large mass of indigent peasantry co-exist, any legal ban on tenancy will remain a dead letter. And in a situation in which employment opportunities are not expanding commensurate with the growth of the work-force, the landowners are in such a strong position that they find it easy to push up their share of the produce. In the context of the social and economic conditions that prevail at present, it is unrealistic to expect a ban on tenancies to be effective. In States like Kerala where the rural poor are politically conscious and well-organized, many landowners keep their land fallow or grow only one crop where two could be grown. They fear that they may lose the land if they lease it out After considering the pros and cons 1 have come to the conclusion that tenancies should be legalized. The revival of tenancies will improve the access of the rural poor to agricultural land leading to enhanced employment and output. I would, however, suggest that in the Bihar plains, eastern Uttar Pradesh and the delta of the Mahanadi, instead of straightway legalizing tenancy, the first step should be to amend the laws on the lines of the West Bengal law for conferring limited rights on share-croppers. Thereafter, an intensive campaign should be mounted for recording the rights of share-croppers on the lines of West Bengal's Operation Barga.

The new leases should be strictly regulated. The lease should be for fixed periods of three to five years and should be renewable after the expiry of the stipulated period. The lease should be in writing and one copy of the document should be lodged with the Gram Panchayat and another with the Taluk office. The rent should not exceed the limit laid down in the law and the owner should be required to grant receipts. Where a farmer leases in land, the combined area of owned and leased in land should not exceed the ceiling limit applicable to him. Even if the law is amended on these lines, the landowners will still be reluctant to lease out their land. For they may harbour the fear of the law being amended again to confer ownership rights on tenants. So it will be necessary to give a solemn assurance that no such amendment will be made in future.

Ceiling on Agricultural Holdings

Despite the dynamism displayed by Indian agriculture and the sustained growth experienced in recent years, the agrarian structure continues to be beset by a host of serious problems. The pressure of population on land continues to rise steadily and there is no hope of a decline in the proportion of the work-force dependent on agriculture in the near future. There is no clear evidence of economies of scale in Indian agriculture. Nor is there any evidence of a positive correlation between increase in the area of the holding and employment. The size-class distribution of land holdings continues to be skewed and the number of small and marginal is growing year by year. In the context of rising agricultural productivity and soaring land prices, there would have been a greater concentration of land in the hands of rich farmers and speculators but for the ceiling laws. If the ceiling laws are relaxed, there will be a scramble for the purchase of land by rich farmers and speculators leading to a further rise in land prices. And the speculators may not be interested in putting the land to intensive use. The small and marginal farmers will find it even more difficult to expand their holdings by buying more land. Considering all these factors I am opposed to the repeal of the ceiling laws. The question of abrogating the ceiling laws can be considered when the rural population dependent on agriculture falls below, say, 2C per cent.

I am also opposed to any further lowering of the ceiling levels. Apart from the fact that a further reduction in the levels of ceiling is not feasible politically, it is also doubtful if it will serve any useful purpose. In future, the State governments should concentrate on the implementation of the existing laws and the quick distribution of the surplus land. Better results can be obtained if attention is concentrated on the large landowners who have successfully evaded the law so far.

Absentee Landowners

One of the principal aims of our land policy should be to take away the operation of agricultural land from the hands of absentee owners who do not take sufficient interest in cultivating their land. The strict enforcement of ceiling law will be of some help in achieving this objective. The legalization of tenancy will also help. But these measures alone will not be enough. Another measure I would propose is the acquisition of the land of absentee landowners under the Land Acquisition Act for distribution to the rural poor.

Land Reform for Growth

Though the role of land reform in removing obstacles to raising agricultural production had been recognized right from the beginning, the greater emphasis was always on its role in leveling down social and economic disparities. During the last five decades, we made a good deal of noise about land reform. Some efforts were also made. But the results have not been commensurate with the noise or the efforts. We have now stopped paying even lip service to the socialist or socialistic ideal. So there is no point in continuing to talk about the role of land reform in ushering in an egalitarian social order. The emphasis should now shift to the role of land reform in fostering agricultural growth and augmenting employment opportunities. Hence the need for revising the land policy.

Land Reforms in India

In India, the rural sector, which accounts for about three-fourths of the country's population, is the mainstay of the majority of the people. For the rural society, land is the most relevant source of living for a large section of the people. The land, however small in area, confers socio-economic status and dignity to the landholders. Land reforms are, therefore, considered to be the very basic programme in the whole range of rural development activities and, accordingly these have been on the national agenda of rural reconstruction since Independence and their need have been constantly recognised in the successive Five Year Plans.

The major objectives of land reforms consist of reordering agrarian relations to achieve an egalitarian social structure; elimination of exploitation in land relations; realising the age-old goal of "land to the tiller"; enlarging the land-base of the rural poor; increasing agricultural productivity and production. These objects have been sought to be achieved by adopting a comprehensive strategy consisting of the following components:

i) Abolition of intermediary tenures;

ii) Tenancy reforms to provide for conferment of ownership, security of tenure and fair rent;

iii) Ceiling on ownership of agricultural holdings and distribution of surplus land to the landless poor;

iv) Distribution of government wastelands including Bhoodan land;

v) Modernisation and updating of land records system for better implementation of land reforms;

vi) Special measures for protection of land of tribals and for restoration of alienated land; and

vii) Consolidation of holdings.

The work relating to abolition of intermediary tenures has been completed and 20 million cultivators have been brought into direct contact with the State. An estimated 150 lakh acres of waste, fallow and other classes of land have been vested in the State.

Tenancy Reforms

Land to the tiller is the accepted national policy and as such tenancy reforms have been considered one of the components of land key reforms. There are incidences of oral and insecure tenancies at will which lead to low investment, tack of stake by the tenants in the land, low productivity leading to severe restraint on the growth process in the rural areas. Factors like absentee landlordism and leaving the land fallow by large and medium landholders lead to general impoverishment of the rural areas. Tenancy reforms, therefore, assume considerable importance.

The following have been the basic objectives of tenancy reforms as outlined in the Five Year Plans and accepted by the government:

(a) Rent should not exceed the level of one-fifth to one-fourth of the gross produce.

(b) There should be security to the subtenants/under-rayats/share-croppers against eviction at will.

(c) The subtenants/under-rayats/share-croppers should enjoy a degree of permanence in respect of the land being cultivated by them.

(d) The landlord tenant relationship, except, in the case of a few categories should end in conferment of the ownership rights upon the tenant.

(e) Tenants should be accorded permanent rights in the land that they cultivate subject to the special right of resumption to be exercised by some privileged categories of landholders.

Legislative provisions have been made in extensive areas of the country providing for conferment of ownership rights on tenants or allowing cultivating tenants to acquire ownership rights on payment of a reasonable compensation to the landlords. Some of the States have acquired ownership of land from the landlords and have transferred it to the tenants who have to pay certain amount of premium to the State. As a result of this, an estimated 112.13 lakh cultivators have been conferred with ownership rights or their rights have been protected on 153.32 lakh acres of land. All tenants are generally protected except for those of widows, members of armed forces, minors, unmarried women, persons suffering from disability and similar categories. Any mention of tenancy reforms would be incomplete if the success achieved in West Bengal is not highlighted wherein under "Operation Barga" a drive launched in the State, to record *Bargadars* (share-croppers). About 14.60 lakh Bargadars were recorded. In view of this spectacular achievement, the Minister of Rural Areas and Employment has urged other States to undertake similar drive so that the interests of tenants/share-croppers are adequately protected.

Ceiling on Agricultural Holdings and Distribution of Ceiling Surplus Land

One of the basic objectives of land reforms is to bring about a more equitable distribution of land. The main instrument for realising this objective was the imposition of ceiling on land. In line with the prescription of the Five Year Plans, laws on imposition of ceiling on agricultural holdings were enacted by several States during the fifties and sixties. The national guidelines on land ceiling were evolved in 1972 after a conference of Chief Ministers. The level of ceiling applicable to a family, as recommended in these guidelines, generally varied from 10 to 18 acres for the best category of land, capable of producing two crops a year to 54 acres of dry land. The State-wise limits of the land ceilings are given in the following Table.

Land Ceilings—State-Wise Limits

(in acres)

State	*Irrigated with 2 crops*	*Irrigated with 1 crop*	*Dry land*
Andhra Pradesh	10-18	15-27	35-54
Assam	17	17	17
Bihar	15-18	25	30-45
Gujarat	10-18	15-27	20-54
Haryana	18	27	54
Himachal Pradesh	10	15	30-70
Jammu & Kashmir	9-12.5	9-12.5	15-23
Karnataka	10-20	25-30	54
Kerala	12-15	12-15	12-15
Madhya Pradesh	18	27	54
Maharashtra	18	27	54
Manipur	12	12	15
Orissa	10	15	30-45
Punjab	17	27	51
Rajasthan	18	27	54-175
Sikkim	12.5	12.5	50
Tamil Nadu	12	30	60
Tripura	10	10	30
Uttar Pradesh	18	27	45
West Bengal	12	12	17

The estimates of surplus area in the country have been arrived at on the basis of certain assumptions which are as follows:

Surplus Land: Estimates

(in lakh acres)

1.	16th Round of NSS (1960-61)	220
2.	Agricultural Census (1970-71)	300
3.	26th Round of NSS (1971-72)	120
4.	Agricultural Census (1976-77)	200
5.	Agricultural Census (1980-81)	150
6.	Agricultural Census (1985-86)	125

The total area so far declared surplus under the programme for distribution of ceiling surplus land is 74.10 lakh acres out of which 65.42 lakh acres have been taken possession of. A total of 51.46 lakh acres have been distributed to 49.94 lakh beneficiaries, of whom 36 per cent belong to the Scheduled Castes and 14 per cent to the Scheduled Tribes.

It would be observed from the above that the extent of area declared surplus is much less than the estimated surplus which is mainly on account of the following reasons:

(a) Provision for holding land up to twice the ceiling limit by families with over five members.

(b) Provision to give separate ceiling limit for major sons in the family.

(c) Provision for treating every shareholder of a joint family under applicable personal law as a separate unit for ceiling limits.

(d) Exemption of tea, coffee, rubber, cardamom and cocoa plantation and of lands held by religious and charitable institutions beyond normal ceiling limits.

(e) Benami and Farzi transfers to defeat the ceiling law.

(f) Misuse of exemptions and misclassifications of land.

(g) Non-application of appropriate ceilings for lands irrigated by public investment.

The subject of distribution of ceiling surplus land has been discussed and reviewed from time to time at various fora including the conferences of Revenue Ministers and Chief Ministers and on the basis of the decisions taken in these conferences, the States are advised to speed up/ reorient their land distribution programme. A special drive for distribution of ceiling surplus land was launched in October 1991 and an area of 3.14 lakh acres was distributed during a short span of two and-a-half years, viz. October, 1991 to March, 1994. The Minister for Rural Areas and Employment also recently focused on the need for expeditious distribution of surplus land by the State governments besides setting up of Land Tribunals under Article 323-B of the Constitution for quick disposal of land ceiling cases.

To assess the impact of the distribution programme on the socio-economic conditions of the allottees, certain systematic studies have been conducted which have revealed that there is certainly an improvement in the social and financial status of the families who were allotted ceiling surplus land. Thus, the purpose and the objective with which the distribution programme was originally launched is being achieved satisfactorily.

Distribution of Government Wasteland and Bhoodan Land

Distribution of government wasteland and Bhoodan land has been one of the important strategies of land reforms. There is approximately 32 million acres of wasteland and 45.90 lakh acres of Bhoodan land in the country. It has been the accepted policy that wasteland at the disposal of the government and the land donated under the Bhoodan movement should be distributed amongst the eligible rural poor. So far, an area of 127.97 lakh acres of wasteland and 24.42 lakh acres of Bhoodan land has been distributed. State governments have been requested to take requisite steps for distribution of all available wasteland and Bhoodan land expeditiously.

Since much of the land distributed under the ceiling laws is of poor quality, the assignees were being provided with financial assistance under a Centrally sponsored scheme at die rate of Rs. 2,500 per hectare. Up to 1992-93, financial assistance by way of grant to the tune of Rs. 59.72 crore as Central share was released to States/Union Territories under the scheme. Now the scheme stands transferred to the State sector. The assignees are, however, accorded priority under other on-going rural development programmes, viz., IRDP and the Jawahar Rozgar Yojana.

Land Records

Updated land records are crucial for implementation of land reform measures and various rural, development programmes. The cause of rural conflicts have often been traced to improper maintenance of land records. It has been noticed that inaccurate land records have become a means of manipulation for influential and powerful sections of the society in order to defeat the progressive provisions of law.

Althou;h the importance of a proper land records system has been emphasised right from the First Five Year Plan, yet land records are in a state of neglect. Even in the States which could boast of a sound land record system in the past, the quality of record keeping and updating has gone down. This is primarily due to the neglect of revenue and land record administration. Allocation of inadequate funds, insufficient staff with unduly large jui isdiction, poor infrastructure and office facilities, lack of equipment, lack of training facilities, etc have contributed to the deterioration of land records administration. The work of preparation and updating of, land records has also been hampered by the use of outdated equipment and high cost and time-consuming methods. The entire survey work is done manually and is highly staff oriented.

Therefore, to assist the States/UTs in the task of updating of land records, a Centrally sponsored scheme for strengthening of revenue administration and updating of land records was started in 1987-88 on 50:50 sharing basis between the Centre and the States. The main objectives of the scheme are:

i) Strengthening of survey and settlement organisation for early completion and preparation of land records in areas where this work still remains to be done;

ii) Setting up of survey and settlement organisation especially in the North-Eastern region, where no land records exist;

iii) Pre-service and in-service training of revenue, survey and settlement staff and strengthening of training infrastructure for this purpose;

iv) Facilities for modernisation of survey and settlement operations, printing of survey maps, reports/ documents and for storage, copying and updating of land and crop records using, among other things, science and technology inputs; and

v) Strengthening of revenue machinery at village and immediate supervisory levels on a selective basis to make the workload of these functionaries manageable.

Since the inception of the scheme, an amount of Rs. 104.73 crore has been allocated to States/UTs towards Central share.

Computerisation: The Land records system currently being followed has remained unchanged since the late 19th century. After Independence, significant structural and tenurial changes have taken place—abolition of intermediary tenures, protection of rights of the tenants, and conferment of ownership to tenants. The programme of land ceiling and consolidation requires dynamic system of land management. It calls for not only greater efficiency in data storage and retrieval but also processing of this data and its integration into the development planning process. The application of computer technology to various fields of administration, particularly in the field of land reforms and land records management will bring in modernisation of this system.

With the above objective in view, 24 districts in the country were selected for implementation of computerisation programme on a pilot project basis. During 1993-94 and 1994-95, the programme was extended to cover 76 more districts. In addition, funds to the UTs have also been provided under the programme. Thus 102 projects have been taken up and an amount of Rs. 24.28 crore has been provided to the States/UTs under this programme.

Committee on Revitalisation of Land Revenue Administration

As stated in the preceding paragraphs land revenue administration has not been receiving the attention it actually deserves. Therefore, in order that the revenue administration is revamped so that it functions as an effective instrument of national development and for fulfilling people's aspirations, the Government of India had appointed a seven-member committee on Revitalisation of Land Revenue Administration under the Chairmanship of Mr P.S. Appu, former Chief Secretary, Government of Bihar, in August, 1993. The Committee submitted its report in March, 1995 and has made a number of recommendations which are expected to go a long way in improving the existing status of land revenue administration in the country. These recommendations are under consideration.

Protection of Tribal Land

Article 46 of the Constitution enjoins an obligation upon the States to promote the interests of the Scheduled Castes and the Scheduled Tribes and to protect them from social injustice and all forms of exploitation.

The major concentration of tribal population is in the States of Bihar, Madhya Pradesh, Orissa, Andhra Pradesh, Rajasthan, and West Bengal, apart from the North-Eastern region. The economy of the tribals continues to be land-based, with agriculture forming the mainstay of the tribal life. This land has been in the process of getting alienated in the wake of migration of population to the tribal areas in search of employment and for exploitation of industrial and job opportunities. There have also been deep incursions into the tribal land and life for the exploitation of the mineral resources, land, labour and industrial activities. This has given rise to severe discontent in the area. It is, therefore, necessary that the land issue which forms the crux of the problem must be effectively attended to.

The State governments have accepted the policy to prohibit transfer of land from tribals to non-tribals and for restoration of the alienated land to the tribals. The States with large tribal population have enacted laws prohibiting alienation of tribal land and for restoration of alienated land. These provisions are, however, generally applicable to the tribals living within the scheduled and notified areas. Though as a consequence of the efforts undertaken by different States for restoration of tribal lands some results have been forthcoming, yet the task still remains unfulfilled. States having tribal population have, therefore, been requested to adopt certain legal, administrative and other socio-economic measures which are crucial to the successful implementation of tribal and rural development programmes so that the interests of the tribals are adequately protected.

Consolidation of Holdings

Consolidation of agricultural holdings is considered necessary for planned development of villages and achieving efficiency and economy in agriculture. The measure assumes added importance in the context that the average size of the operational holdings in the country is very low and these undersized holdings are highly fragmented. This programme, therefore, forms an integral part of land reforms policy and the Five Year Plans have accordingly been laying stress on the importance of its implementation. In pursuance of this strategy, a number of States have enacted legislation for, carrying out consolidation of holdings but all of them have not pursued its implementation with equal vigour.

Fifteen States and two Union Territories, viz. Andhra Pradesh (Telengana area), Assam, Bihar, Gujarat, Haryana, Himachal Pradesh, Jammu and Kashmir, Karnataka, Madhya Pradesh, Maharashtra, Orissa, Punjab, Rajasthan, Uttar Pradesh, West Bengal, Delhi and Dadra and Nagar Haveli have legislative provisions for undertaking consolidation of holdings. The Andhra area of Andhra Pradesh, Goa, Kerala, Manipur, Tamil Nadu and Tripura do not have law for undertaking such operations. Conditions in the north-eastern States like Arunachal Pradesh, Meghalaya, Mizoram and Nagaland do not offer sufficient scope for consolidation. In Sikkim also, 80 per cent of the land holdings are such that they do not require consolidation.

Andhra Pradesh, Jammu and Kashmir, Karnataka and Rajasthan had undertaken consolidation work earlier but presently there is no scheme in operation in these States. In Bihar, Gujarat, Haryana, Himachal Pradesh, Madhya Pradesh, Maharashtra, Orissa, Punjab, Uttar Pradesh, and Delhi the consolidation of holdings is either currently or till recently was in progress. Of these States, Bihar, Haryana, Orissa, Punjab, Uttar Pradesh and Delhi have provisions for compulsory consolidation while in Gujarat and Maharashtra, though the provisions provide for compulsory consolidation, in practice the scheme is undertaken on a voluntary basis. In Madhya Pradesh, the scheme is voluntary.

Consolidation of holdings has, however, made great impact in Punjab, Haryana and Uttar Pradesh, while in Bihar, Orissa, Maharashtra and Himachal Pradesh it has been taken up in large areas. Around 1556.12 lakh acres of land have so far been consolidated in the country. The States where this programme is being implemented have been advised to make adequate arrangements to ensure that the interests of small and marginal farmers and tenants and share-croppers are fully protected in the process of consolidation of agricultural holdings to enlist their active co-operation. However, there are certain factors which work against the consolidation of holdings, e.g. fear of displacement among tenants and share-croppers, apprehension that bigger farmers would get a better deal, specially when lands are not homogenous etc.

The benefits of consolidation have no effect if the process of fragmentation by inheritance and otherwise goes on unabated. Many States do have provisions in the State laws for prevention of fragmentation but these mostly regulate transfer and partition but do not govern inheritance. The Eighth Five Year Plan document has, therefore, laid emphasis ob the need for attention on the following two aspects:

(a) The smaller farmers harbour strong apprehensions about getting a raw deal in the process of exchanging parcels of land towards the consolidation of holdings; and

(b) The process of breaking up of holdings is a continuous one and a one-time settlement does not really solve the problem.

The Plan document, therefore, suggests that the solution will be in making the farmer recognise that it is advantageous to share income from land rather than the land itself. The modality of bringing these aims into the land related customs and practices will be more effective than the passing of laws.

Since consolidation has not made much headway in many of the States and in some States not even its feasibility has been considered so far, the Minister (Rural Areas & Employment), therefore, recently stressed the need for effec tive implementation of this programme by the State governments.

Though land reform measures so far undertaken have, no doubt, yielded considerable success, yet a lot more is required to be done particularly to speed up the implementation of the programme as still a large chunk of ceiling surplus as well as wasteland and Bhoodan land is yet to be distributed, a substantial amount of ceiling surplus area is locked in litigation at various levels, concealed tenancies are still in vogue, the position of land record system continues to be unsatisfactory, alienation of tribal land is going on unabated and large areas in various States need to be consolidated.

Needless to say that land is a State subject and accordingly, it is the State governments who are actually executing the policies and programmes on land reforms. The Government of India has an advisory and co-ordinating role to perform in the implementation of land reform programmes. Though, the States are fully co-operating and implementing the land reform measures with all their earnestness, yet it is felt that some more thrust is needed for effective and expeditious implementation of the land reform policy in the country so that the benefits accrued therefrom reach the target group. The Ministry of Rural Areas and Employment is, therefore, advising the States from time to time on various aspects of land reforms and also suggesting action plan for achieving the objectives of the policy. The Ministry is also closely monitoring the progress in this regard. Also, for giving further fillip to the programme, conferences of Revenue Secretaries, Revenue Ministers and Chief Ministers are organised from time to time where the progress made under various components of the land reform policy is reviewed and the States and other agencies concerned are advised on the steps necessary" for effective implementation of the land reform measures.

2

Effective Implementation of Land Reforms: Need of the Hour

Land Reforms have continued to be on the national agenda of rural reconstruction since Independence. It has been viewed as a measure of redistributive justice and as a means to achieving higher levels of agricultural production and incomes of the rural areas. It is a well-accepted fact that given the present stage of agricultural technology, even a small farm can be viable, both in terms of employment and income of a family. The need for land reforms was recognised at the time of Independence and has been reiterated in the successive Five Year Plans. The Seventh Five Year Plan included land reforms as an intrinsic part of the anti-poverty strategy.

Considerable Progress

At the national level, successive Five Year Plans have emphasised abolition of intermediaries, security of tenure of tenant cultivators, redistribution of land by imposition of ceiling on agricultural holdings, consolidation of holdings and updating of land records as important tenets of land reforms. Since land is a State subject, appropriate legislation incorporating most of these issues have been enacted by the State governments. Today when we take stock of what has been achieved in the sphere of land reforms, it is seen that land reforms as a strategy of agricultural development and for achieving the objective of an egalitarian pattern of society, has made considerable progress.

Most States have passed legislation abolishing intermediary tenures like Zamindari, Jagirdari, Inams and other tenures, as also the rent receiving interests of landlords, thus, bringing an estimated 20 million cultivators in direct relationship with the State. Occupancy or ownership rights were conferred on the tenants or cultivators of the land in pursuance of the government's policy of 'land to the tiller'. As a result of the abolition of Zamindari, 40 per cent of the land covered under this system was freed. Fifteen million acres of wasteland were also vested in the States. However, old Zamindars succeeded in retaining large tracts for self-cultivation.

Providing Security to Tenants

Except the States of Meghalaya, Nagaland and Mizoram, all the States had tenancy laws at the time of the Eighth Five Year Plan. These provide for conferring of ownership on the tenants by the State, acquisition of ownership by tenants on payment of reasonable compensation, security of tenure and fixation of fair rent. The national policy in this regard has been that the rent payable to the land-owner should not exceed one-fifth to one-fourth of the gross produce; tenants should be given permanent rights to the land they cultivate subject to a limited right of resumption to be given to landowners and that landlord-tenants relationships should be ended by conferring ownership rights on tenants in respect of non-resumable land. Certain categories such as widows, members of armed forces, minors, etc. are treated separately under these laws.

In certain other cases, provision is also made for a limited right of resumption. An estimated 112.92 lakh cultivators have been conferred ownership rights on 153.53 lakh acres of land.

The experience of implementation of these laws has been quite varied. West Bengal, Kerala and Karnataka, have achieved more success than the other States. The West Bengal model of 'Operation Barga' under which 14.60 lakh share-croppers have been recorded, has provided a replicable model for recording tenancies and securing the rights of tenants and share-croppers. Karnataka has set up land tribunals to settle tenancy issues. These have decided in favour of about three lakh tenants involving approximately 11 lakh acres of land. In Kerala, through the tenants' association applications of 24 lakh tenants for conferment of ownership were accepted.

Due to a loose definition of 'personal cultivation' in most States the tenancy laws have not been able to have the desired impact as the land owners continued to resume the land. Concealed and oral tenancies still continue to exist. The States have been advised to bring all the oral tenants and the share-croppers on record with the help of local Panchayats and voluntary agencies working in these areas. Thus, providing security to these category tenants is one of the most important issues of agrarian reforms today.

Limited Success

Fixation of ceiling on agricultural holdings was taken up as a redistributive measure. The skewed distribution of land in India, with nearly a quarter of the rural households owning no land at all, and another one-fifth owning less than an acre each, provided ample social and economic reason for land ceiling as a means of redressing this imbalance. Legislation for ceiling on existing holdings and future acquisition were enacted in most States during the Second Plan period. Considering the differences in the legislation of the States, national guidelines were evolved in 1972. Except Goa and in the North-East region, ceiling legislation has been enacted in accordance with these guidelines. The land ceiling programme has suffered due to various loopholes and complexities in the legislation, lack of administrative effort and inadequate and inaccurate land records base. A limited success has been achieved in this programme with total area declared surplus up to March, 1995 being 74.09 lakh acres out of which 65.42 lakh acres have been taken possession of. An area of 51.46 lakh acres has been distributed to 49.94 lakh beneficiaries. This issue was considered by the Revenue Ministers and the Chief Ministers in their conference held in March, 1992 and October, 1992 respectively. The measures suggested to strengthen this programme include :

(1) Setting up of tribunals to take up land ceiling cases;

(2) Freeing 75 per cent of land involved in litigation, and making it available for distribution;

(3) Survey of benami and farzi transactions; and

(4) Computerisation of land records.

As mere allotment of ceiling surplus land does not ensure a proper and optimum utilisation by the allottees, a Centrally sponsored scheme for providing financial assistance to the assignees of ceiling surplus land, SC/ST allottees of Bhoodan land and government wastelands, and SC/ST who had been restored their alienated land after 1 April, 1985, was in operation from 1975-76 to 1992-93, after which it has been transferred to the States. In this scheme, an assistance of Rs. 2,500 per hectare is given to the beneficiary for land development, purchase of inputs and for meeting consumption needs.

Consolidation of Holdings & Security of Tenure

Consolidation of holdings is necessary for efficiency and economy in agriculture and better development planning at the village level. It has been implemented successfully in some States like Punjab, Haryana, and Uttar Pradesh where differences in the quality of land and availability of irrigation facilities were minimal, so that the farmers did not fear exchange of lands in the process of consolidation. It has been seen that consolidation of holdings has generally suffered in its progress because of the apprehensions of small farmers about getting a raw-deal in exchanging parcels of land for a consolidated holding. Since the process of fragmentation of holdings, is a continuous one, a one-time activity will not solve this problem. Attempts have to be made to convince the farmer that this measure will lead to an increase in agricultural production, in resolving land-based conflicts and will bring better harmony and social facilities to village life. In allaying the fears and apprehensions of the tenants and share-croppers, measures for tenancy reforms to give security of tenure to tenants are a pre-requisite before an effective programme of consolidation of land holdings can be implemented. It has been taken up in large areas of Bihar, Orissa, Maharashtra and Himachal Pradesh. Whereas, Andhra Pradesh, (Telengana area) and Assam have enacted legislative provisions for consolidation of land holdings. Tamil Nadu, Kerala and other North-Eastern States do not have any laws for this purpose. Some of the States have given it a voluntary character. Around 1528.76 lakh acres of land have been consolidated in the country so far.

Wasteland and Bhoodan Land

There is approximately 320 million acres of wasteland in the country. So far, an area of 127.97 lakh acres of wasteland has been distributed. In a number of States, it has been observed in many instances that allottees of government wastelands have not been found in possession of the land given to them. In the case of Bhoodan land, as the original donations were made 25-30 years ago, the records of the donation are not available and the heirs of the original donees have challenged the donations. Of the 45.90 lakh acres of land donated as Bhoodan land, only 24.42 lakh acres have been distributed. A survey of Bhoodan lands and government wasteland available, should be made and priority given to distribution of these lands to SCs/STs. States like Andhra Pradesh, Madhya Pradesh, Uttar Pradesh and Orissa have performed well in the distribution of Bhoodan land.

Updating Land Records

The Government of India has recognised the fact that in most cases land records are not up-to-date and even where land records are regularly maintained, the ground reality is often not reflected in them, particularly, regarding tenancy and share-croppers. Some States, specially, in the North-East do not have any land records system and neither have they been able to find sufficient resources to get the land resurveyed and get the records updated. The present state of affairs has arisen due to an inadequate machinery for regular updating of land records and insufficient financial provisions for this purpose from amongst the States' resources. The archaic system of preparing land records and updating them is reflected in their poor upkeep. Recognising the need for updating the land records and for following methods of modern technology, a Centrally sponsored scheme for strengthening of revenue administration and updating of land records was begun from 1987-88 during the Seventh Five Year Plan. In this scheme, assistance is provided to the States for induction of modern technology in the maintenance and updating of land records, purchase of equipment, strengthening of training of personnel, infrastructure, etc. An amount of Rs. 96.91 crore had been released by the Central government as its share to the States/UTs between 1987-88 and 1994-95.

Computerisation: A pilot project for computerisation of land records was initiated in 1989. Since 1993-94, a Centrally sponsored scheme with 100 per cent Central assistance has been launched for computerisation of land records. Projects in 102 districts in the country have been sanctioned till 1994-95. One hundred new projects are proposed to be taken up during the current year. The experience of the States has been varied in the implementation of this scheme.

The other components of the strategy of land reforms which require special mention are: conferment of ownership of rights on homeless persons, taking special measure for protection of lands of SCs and STs, improving the access of land to women, and safeguarding of common property resources.

Eighth Plan Strategy

The Eighth Plan aims at addressing itself to the factors that have come in the way of realising the goals of land reforms policy. It lays stress on ensuring that the actual cultivators are made aware of their rights and are enabled to claim their benefits. It also aims at encouraging steps for early detection of surplus land. The Eighth Plan recognises that the newly acquired land has to be brought under profitable agronomic practices to meet the twin objectives of poverty-alleviation and output growth. The management of land records and the skills and capabilities of the lower level machinery thus becomes important and needs the necessary support of resources and modernisation so that they help rather than hinder evolution of an equitable agrarian order.

Reward System: In order to create a reward system for the better performing States in these matters, an index of performance with regard to land records, has been set up which has been included in the Modified Gadgil Formula. Based on this indicator, it is possible to provide a portion of the general pool of Central assistance to the States.

Security of Tenants: The Eighth Plan has highlighted issues relating to security of tenants:

First, there is a need of solidarity among the tenants so that they can counter the dominance of landed classes as well as make the revenue administration accountable to themselves.

Secondly, transfer of title to the actual cultivators requires to be professional and sensitive.

Thirdly, it is important to ensure that the allottees receive the gains from the land with the help of improved technology and modern inputs.

Restricting the right to resumption, tackling absentee landlordism by defining personal cultivation more precisely and reviewing the provisions for regulating voluntary surrender are some of the issues highlighted in the Eighth Plan in the national perspective. There is also a need for organisation of tenants and share-croppers to assist in the detection of informal and concealed tenancies and to bring on records tenants and share-croppers.

Detecting Surplus Land: There is a need to detect surplus lands which have been unavailable due to evasive methods till now. It is also incumbent upon the State governments to take measures to ensure that the allottees take possession and there is severe penalty for dispossession. This may require certain amendments in the law to remove the lacunae.

Common Property Resources and NGOs

The question of common property resources, which have traditionally been a source of economic sustenance for the weaker sections of the society, is also engaging the attention of the policy-makers and planners. It is necessary to survey the extent of the common property resources in the rural areas and to remove encroachments by more influential sections, so as to increase their access to the weaker sections. This is another area where voluntary organisations and local democratic institutions have to be associated with the administrative machinery.

PRIs and Land Reforms

The process of democratic decentralisation and empowerment of local government institutions in the rural areas, has been given a constitutional status by the Constitution (73rd Amendment) Act, 1992. The scope of involving the Panchayati Raj Institutions in the implementation of land reforms, has to be discussed and formalised in concrete terms. The 11th Schedule to the Constitution includes implementation of land reforms, land consolidation, land improvement and soil conservation as items of work which may be transferred to these institutions by the State governments through statutory provisions. Referring to the experience of Operation Barga of West Bengal, there is a strong case for involving these local democratic institutions in ttfiswrocess so as to achieve the goals of the land reforms policy.

The Slow Progress of Land Reforms in India

The principal upthrust of all policy measures in India has been to eradicate mass poverty. And since an overwhelming proportion of Indian population lives in villages, it has naturally meant focusing on how rural transformation can also help achieve this aim.

While people in the rural areas engage themselves in non-agricultural activities as well for a living, agriculture is the axis around which all those activities revolve. So the peasant is really the pivotal producer and land is the most crucial factor of his production. What net return cultivation leaves him with is thus the stimulus which determines whether he will put in his best effort and thus influence his own and everybody else's well-being in terms of adequate supply of food and raw materials. Agriculture may be a way of life for him but incentive is needed to enthuse him with a greater sense of dynamism.

Absentee Landlordism

It is with such a rationale as this that the concern for land reform had begun to appear in India even during the freedom struggle. Since freedom, the concern has been translated into a number of steps including policy decisions and their implementation so that the objective of "land to the tiller" could be achieved. However, while landlordism has been abolished, we still have a new type of 'absentee landlordism', substantial amount of temporary tenancy and subtenancy in which the needy sections of poor peasantry have to part sometimes with 50 to 66 per cent of the produce to their landowners. Thus, though in the wake of Zamindari abolition more than 20 million tenants of zamindari land had by 1961 become directly related to the State, and the zamindars were deprived of 60 per cent of whatever land they had, the poor peasantry still continued to be exploited. In eastern UP, informal subletting embraced 29 per cent of the net cultivated area when formal subletting was shown to cover one per cent only. The landholders involved were 17 per cent of the total.

It is obvious that informal tenancy enables the owners to charge higher rents and makes for even more severe exploitation of the peasants.

Variations in Rents

Attempts at regulating rents have been made with variations ranging from one-third of the gross produce in Punjab and 33.3 to 40 per cent in Tamil Nadu, a maximum of one-sixth in Gujarat, Maharashtra and Rajasthan and one-fourth to one-fifth in Assam, Karnataka, Manipur and Tripura. The likelihood of rents exceeding these limits becomes stronger the greater the extent of informal tenancy.

Another factor which could be helpful to peasants involved in informal or oral tenancy would be fixing rents in money and discouraging payments in kind, since payment in kind in situations of continuing inflation would benefit the receivers of rent more than the giver. Moreover, when many other payments which the peasant makes are in money, why should this also not be paid in money rather in kind?

The Way Out

A secure right of tenancy had rightly been considered as a way out of the problem. One usual technique of the landowners has been to threaten resumption of self-cultivation and thus create helplessness for the share-croppers. To counter the tendency, UP, Delhi and West Bengal have provided for full security of tenure to tenants and no right of personal cultivation to the owners. But most States—Madhya Pradesh, Rajasthan, Himachal Pradesh, Orissa, Maharashtra, Gujarat, Kerala, Assam and Punjab have provided for resumption of cultivation of a limited area with a minimum area being left with the tenant. Tripura, Manipur, Jammu and Kashmir allow for a limited resumption of cultivation by landowners but there is no entitlement to the tenant for a minimum for his own cultivation.

Assuming that about 20 per cent of the tenants hold oral leases, the extent of rack-renting and insecurity of tenure could make more than a marginal difference to the output in the agricultural sector and to the poverty and economic well-being of the affected peasants.

Security of Tenure: The steps taken thus far to provide security of tenure and prevent charging of extortionist rents have been all in the right direction, the inter-State differences notwithstanding, but the larger issues of political will, bureaucratic apathy, dilatory judicial processes handicap their speedy implementation. The same forces might be holding back straightening and finalising of land records without which targeting the exploiters is even more difficult.

Ceiling Limits: Variations

We will revert to the basic issues presently. Meanwhile, we might refer to that related matter of ceiling on land-holdings which was intended to yield a surplus over ceiling, which could then be distributed to poor peasants and landless labourers in the country.

The ceiling unit which was the landholder himself until 1972, was changed to the family thereafter. However, the family unit's definition with husband, wife and three minor children leaves scope for a large variation in the ceiling if major children are allowed as large a land additionally as the family excluding them is allowed. The ceiling limits were also lowered thereafter with differences varying as between irrigated land with two crops, irrigated land with one crop and dry land. The exemptions for orchards, grazing land, cattle breeding farms, religious trusts, orchards, sugar-cane farms, etc. have all tended to vary the ceiling and raise it substantially in many cases.

Problems Galore

The surplus over ceiling available for distribution to small farmers, evicted tenants and the landless has been less than warranted because of various malpractices, checkmating of which is obviously administration's responsibility. However, the fulfilment of that responsibility is caught up in the general political milieu and again brings us back to the basic issues.

But problems of compensation to those whose surplus land is being acquired and recovery of this amount from those who are being given this land fall in a somewhat different category. These problems have both economic and legal aspects. The economic aspect arises from whether the small holder's return would be enough to provide for both the rent and the payment of the value of land acquired. The legal aspect could arise from whether the compensation meets the satisfaction of the party whose land is being taken away. That the latter has remained interested in involving surplus in litigation is confirmed by the fact that in comparison to the surplus land that is supposed to be left for distribution, some eleven times that land is already involved in litigation!

Need for political will: The issue of the burden of distributed land's price on the smallholder could be resolved within a time-horizon in which the annual land revenue the produce and instalment of land's price put together do not exceed the proportion of output statutorily chargeable as land revenue in the area. Evidently, this will mean that land revenue charged from the smallholder will be less than the statutory maximum. This would have fiscal implication which would need to be sorted out in terms of larger policy considerations. And like many other issues having fiscal implications, this will also have to depend on political will of the governments concerned.

The steps emphasised on a priority basis have been either shortening the judicial processes in relation to land reforms through setting up of special tribunals or benches of High Courts or through curtailing the powers of the judiciary in the matter. At least Ssection 323 of the Constitution provides for the former and there is no reason why we should not take advantage of that provision.

Land records: The necessity of maintaining proper lane records has always been felt and particularly since the success of West Bengal's Operation Barga, which is being widely commended. In fact, the Centre has provided for Rs. 24.48 crore for computerisation of land records and even otherwise, it is agreeable to share expenditure incurred or improving land records and revenue administration.

Efforts are also being made so that government avoids laying its own hands on surplus land and enables its distribution to the poorer sections of the rural population. There is also the suggestion to change laws in a manner that the tribals are not deprived of their land and in case their land.

PRIs: A Ray of Hope?

With the Panchayats taking up position now, a chapter of hope on land reforms opens though it is unclear if issues like tardiness of the judicial process, the distortion of ceiling through manipulation of vested interests, the lack of political and administrative will, absence of comprehensive land records including those relating to *batai* or share-cropping would really be effectively tackled at the level of individual Panchayats. And where resource constraint is also a factor proving a handicap in the way of land reforms, it is particularly unclear how Panchayats would go about the problem.

Until now there is no indication how Panchayats will raise their resources and if they don't, how the Centre or the States are going to bail them out.

In this connection, one could refer to possibilities of action on a suggestion which has been frequently made, namely the desirability of organising the rural poor and the landless so that they can force the emergence of a political will to implement land reforms seriously. Could Panchayats help forge such an organisation? Even if they did, will it be effective on a purely local, micro level?

Already there is increasing tendency to fight Panchayat elections too under known party banners and there is no evidence that any party or group articulating the interests of the rural poor is anywhere around. As for the existing parties, they are so anchored to the goal of just capturing political power that they hardly find time for focusing on the plight of the landless and the rural poor.

Social Justice and Economic Growth

Does the approach of social justice through land reforms militate against the objective of economic growth in the agricultural sector?

The question would not have been raised when the case for land reforms started gathering momentum both in the pre-Independence and in the immediately post-Independence era. At that time, social justice was considered necessary for maximisation of economic growth in the economy as a whole and agriculture was no exception to an already widely held opinion in the country. But when the growth process began, vested interests saw great opportunities for maximisation of personal gain so that wherever they were, in the private corporate sector, public sector, political br administrative sector or the agricultural sector, they played up growth and played down distributive justice, so much so that even Pandit Nehru had to say that rather than distribute poverty we should first produce wealth and then bother about its distribution. Slowly but surely the general ethos began to slide back from social justice to just removal of poverty and it is no surprise, therefore, if in such an ethos the political will, weak even though it was at the best of times, began to get continually emasculated.

And so in the process, the fact that smaller farms were yielding better value added also began to be overlooked.

At least from the point of view of efficiency of production and growth of agricultural output, the bias in favour of redistribution and encouraging smaller farms could not be faulted.

Nor could the scale argument go far with the kind of technological change we have fruitfully ushered in the realm of agricultural production. The technology admits of a fairly high degree of divisibility of inputs and that is why the combination of that technology and self-employed labour enables the achievement of a higher value added on farms of smaller size.

Why is, then, there a demand now for raising land ceiling even from States like West Bengal? Because they say or would attract the private sector and make more resources available for the agricultural investment.

Liberalisation and Agricultural Sector

It is common knowledge that the total investment in agriculture has gone down in the wake of liberalisation. It is difficult for any government to concede such ill-consequences of its policy. On the other hand, the States are yet to do anything substantial to boost resources and make up the deficiency in agricultural investment. From inefficiency and lack of dynamism of public sector to the supposed opposite traits of the private sector, we may have made a directional movement which has left people guessing, some with optimism and hope and some with pessimism and disappointment. But it is entirely unclear how with a persistent sluggishness in the savings to national income ratio, a more unbridled consumerism in the wake of liberalisation and a sustained effort to run away from taxation and, therefore, a declining pool of national resources, the private sector would find resources which the public sector would not. And if that is unclear, how can the argument be used to reverse the basic thinking which has underlined our land reform programme thus far?

The question: The really likely possibility on the front of resources at least in the new economic policy scenario is to fish from the global rather than from the national pool of resources. But if that led to the possibility of foreign private participation in agriculture as is happening and is being sought to be encouraged in industry, will that strengthen or weaken the political resolve to push ahead with land reforms is the question?

True, the Government of India still continues to make noises about land reforms and against any raising of ceiling. But what does it have to offer by way of substantial resources except the advice that the States must put their fiscal house in order and try to raise themselves by their bootstraps—an advice which the Centre itself has to heed in view of its high fiscal deficit, high level of internal and external debts and the consequential high debt-servicing.

The purpose behind linking land reforms with the issue of resources for agricultural investment is both to point to a newly emerging anti-land reforms situation and to indicate how basic macro-approaches to economic policy could themselves imperceptibly accentuate the prejudices of the judiciary, the bureaucrats and the politicians. Thus understood, their prejudices may be less of a problem than the repeated attempts of economic policy to play down social justice which in turn, then, feed the prejudices. More specifically, the problem may be the creation of an ethos in which pampering to the vested interests of the rich itself begins to be regarded as the best means of achieving social justice.

Whither Land Reforms?

There is still occasional talk of land reforms. Conferences too are periodically held by the Central and State governments where early completion of land reforms is urged. This is done primarily to put of the out of the way a sore problem for official set-up to feel free and comfortable to devote itself to plans to give new, "modern" outlook to Indian agriculture. What is causally missed, however, is the tragic fact that failure to carry out radical land reforms has been the major factor in frustrating the plans for economic growth and social equity during even the era of planning. Under the regime of market-friendly structural adjustment of the Indian economy, the position is not likely to be any different. It, in fact, is likely to aggravate. The attempts, being made ingeniously, rather insidiously, to side-track the fundamental issue of land reform are indeed misconceived and even dangerous.

Agricultural Census

The first and only Agricultural Census in India was released in December 1978. It threw up valuable data on land relations in the agricultural sector of the economy. It showed that medium and large operational holdings covered more land under cultivation than the medium and large categories of farmowners. The position has since worsened because of increasing alienation of marginal farmer from land and greater concentration of farm land in large operational holdings. There were in 1970-71, 70 million operational holdings on an aggregate area of 162 million ha. Of these, 35 million, or one-half, were of a size less than one ha which covered only nine per cent of the total cultivated area. A 1953-55 survey had earlier found that 50 per cent of all small holdings accounted for 10.5 per cent of the total cultivated area. Thus, marginal holdings were found to be losing land. At the other extreme, holdings of 10 ha and increase in the number of operational holdings during this period was of the order of 40 per cent. It meant that fragmentation of land holdings had gone on and land had passed out of the hands of small holders, making them smaller still. It was since the mid-sixties when official policy started to promote commercial agriculture. But ironically enough, at about the time, imposition of ceiling and land redistribution too were mooted.

Dwindling Surplus Land

The first round of ceiling laws, however, resulted in the distribution of only 0.5 million ha when during the same period an additional 38 million ha of land had been brought under cultivation. The redistribution of only half-a-million ha under the ceiling laws could hardly change the land ownership and land holdings pattern in the country, when land redistribution was first mooted in the mid-fifties, it was calculated that with ceiling put at 20 standard acres, 35 million ha of surplus land would become available for redistribution among the poor peasantry. The surplus for redistribution has since eroded at a fast pace. In 1970-71, even with lowering of the ceiling, it was estimated that only 20 million ha were available for redistribution.

Subsequently, the estimates did not go beyond 7.5 lakh ha as the possible surplus land under ceiling laws. The latest is that hardly 40,000 ha are left to be redeemed for redistribution to the poor peasants. The ceiling laws have thus failed miserably to bring about a meaningful change in ownership pattern of land and social relations in the countryside.

Rich Farmers and Idle Land

A finding of the agricultural workers, if given even a small parcel of land, will bring it under cultivation. They will put their family labour on it to eke out at least subsistence from such land. This is indeed the most economic way for the utilisation of available land including what is classified as wasteland, as well as improving employment opportunities in the country. The fact is that gentlemen farmers do not display any interest in bring wasteland under cultivation and do not make investment especially from their own resources for this purpose. They prefer it to lie waste. They too prefer to maximise their profits from trading and usurious operations rather than improve production and productivity per acre of their holdings.

Landless Agricultural Labourers

Another important development in the countryside, because of the miserable failure to carry out land reforms, in particular land redistribution has been the growth in the number of agriculture labourers which had swelled to 29.98 per cent of the rural population by 1970-71 from 18.87 per cent a decade earlier. This happened because of alienation of the poor farmer from land and concentration in land ownership. The number of owner-cultivators, side by side, declined from 60.32 per cent to 50.88 per cent in 1970. These trends have further accentuated, the periodic talk of land reforms and ceiling laws notwithstanding.

The landless agricultural labourers who are estimated to number 160 million at present and poor peasants who after losing their uneconomic parcels of land, may still hanker after land for cultivation. But it has become clear enough that the principal issue for them now is one of wages—fair wages, that is. But they have also to reckon with strong feudalistic forms and practices that still govern social relations in the rural sector and the widespread unemployment in rural area in the absence of alternative avenues of gainful jobs for them in industry or the services sector.

A Contradiction

This broadly is the position with respect to land relations in the agricultural sector. The nature and relevance of the much-advertised new agricultural policy launched in the mid-sixties, which is applauded for ushering in the Green Revolution, has to be examined in the light of the given pattern of land ownership, operational holdings and social relations in this sector. The new agriculture strategy frankly aimed at the promotion of commercial agriculture. By its very nature, it relied on the use of "modern" methods of agriculture. Priority was given to the application of material inputs, among them costly chemical fertilisers and pesticides rather than human labour and inputs that could be generated within the farm sector, among them organic manures. It was limited to selected farm and geographical areas and restricted sections of farmers—the rich fanners and the landed gentry in particular, who had been clamouring precisely for such a dispensation after the end of the Zamindari system. The need and the compulsion for radical land reforms as a factor in lifting agriculture as a whole out of stagnation inevitably lost its rationale in an increasing measure under the new policy orientation.

Social and Political Tension

The concept of land reforms and redistribution of land on the basis of the principle of "land for the tiller" implies reliance on the poorer strata of peasantry, spreading out the network of assistance for farming over a larger and wider scale and unleashing of mass enthusiasm to get greater production through intensive labour mobilisation and utilisation of inputs readily available to them. Chemical fertilisers and pesticides and mechanisation has in this scheme of things to be introduced gradually, naturally, not as a crach programme as was stipulated as the first condition for promoting commercial agriculture in India. The Indian agricultural policy, from the days of the freedom struggle and after Independence, was, however, conceived with a socially broad-based approach to farming. It did not succeed as well as it might have to dramatically increase production and consumption of basic necessities of life for the mass of the people and wage goods for working people, not because it was inherently faulty but because it was not implemented with dedication and efficiency. But it might be right and proper to stress that, even with limitations, it had resulted in increasing agricultural production to an impressive extent. In respect of food grains, for instance, production increased from less than 60 million tonnes at the start of the fifties to nearly 88 million tonnes by 1967-68. A lot more could be achieved if the obstructions of vested interests had been overcome and policy and administrative instruments properly mobilised. It too is worth noting that the operation of the agricultural strategy to promote commercial agriculture since the mid-sixties has recorded an increase in food grains production at a rate not faster than in the previous period. An encouraging factor has been large public investment in irrigation till the mid-seventies, after which there has been deceleration in this crucial investment in agriculture. Benign nature, by way of good monsoons for seven years in a row too has helped. However, the advance of commercial agriculture has pushed large areas and a majority of peasantry to stagnation and decay. It has consolidated the grip of the rich peasant and the landlord on economic activity, social relations, even political alignments, in the rural areas of the country. These trends in the direction of rural development at a crucial stage of the development of the national economy was bound to have serious repercussions for the entire course of social and political life in India. Not only the much talked of egalitarian objective has tended to be made meaningless but any step towards this goal even in future has become more difficult. This is a state of affairs which is prone to inflame social and political tensions such as have tended often to erupt in the last two decades and assume violent forms and features.

Land to the Tiller: A Mirage

It is not amiss, therefore, to recall the 1973 report of the Task Force on Agrarian Relations. It was a strikingly candid document.

It said: "Enactment of progressive measures of land reforms and their efficient implementation call for hard political decisions and effective political support, direction and control. In the context of the socio-economic conditions prevailing in the field of land reform in the absence of the requisite political will, the sad truth is that this crucial factor has been wanting. The lack of political will is amply demonstrated by the large gaps between policy and legislation and between law and its implementation. In no sphere of public activity in our country since Independence has the hiatus between precept and practice, between policy pronouncements and actual execution, been as great as in the domain of land reforms. With resolve and unambiguous political will, all other shortcomings and difficulties could have been overcome; in the absence of such will even minor obstacles become formidable road blocks in the path of the Indian land reform. Considering the character of the political power structure obtaining in the country, it was only natural that the required political will was not forthcoming".

Referring in particular to the objective of "land to the tiller", the report said that this objective will never be achieved in the prevailing conditions of our society and polity.

Failures Galore

The official land reform programme has indeed never been for "land to the tiller". What was done in the direction was aimed at the reduction in the "incidence of absentee ownership of land". The definition of "personal cultivation" in land laws, therefore, turned out to be a major factor in large-scale ejectment of tenants from land and making them agricultural labourers. The abolition of statutory zamindari system in the fifties helped to bring about 20 million intermediate tenants into direct contact with the State and large areas of privately-owned forest land, grazing land and cultivable wasteland was vested in the State. But a compensation, of about Rs. 600 crore for the Zamindars too was provided for. Even so, abolition of the Zamindari system could have made some positive impact on rural life and the agrarian structure with suitable follow-up action. But there was afterwards dithering over tenancy reforms and failure to enforce ceiling on holdings and redistribution of land by legislation sans empowerment of the poor peasantry which nullified this hopeful outcome. The economic and social relations in the countryside have, therefore, actually worsened since the mid-sixties. While tenancy reforms and ceiling on land are known to have failed miserably, the report of the Task Force on Agrarian Relations pointed out that even consolidation of holdings worked to strengthen the landowners' position and weaken that of the tenant and the actual cultivator. About consolidation of holdings, for instance, the Task Force said:

"A major weakness of the programme was that consolidation was done without taking effective steps to ensure security of tenure to tenants, particularly sharecroppers. The result, consolidation of holdings has led to large-scale ejectment of tenants. For one thing, when holdings were fragmented even a resident landowner found it difficult to cultivate personally all the plots of land constituting his fragmented holdings and therefore, perforce he had to lease out some portions of his holdings to sharecroppers. After the holdings were consolidated, the landowner found it both feasible and profitable to cultivate 'personally' the entire area and he spared no effort to get rid of the sharecroppers. For another, the relationship of sharecropping tenancy subsisted in respect of a specific plot of land easily identified in the field. Once consolidation was effected, the identity of the particular plot that the sharecropper had been cultivating was lost and he could be automatically ousted from the land. Thus the consolidation of holdings has often turned out to be the coup de grace for the sharecroppers."

Agrarian and Social Relations: PRI's Role

It is futile, however, to talk of political will coming into play in abstract terms. The fact to be reckoned with is that those who are wielding political power belong, by and large, to landed interests and like them many in the higher echelons of the administration are still substantial landowners themselves or they have close links with big landowners. It is imperative, therefore, that a new administrative machinery must evolve effectively to formulate and implement any worthwhile programme for land reforms. This requires "a certain degree of politicialisation of the poor peasantry on militant lines" as the Task Force on Agrarian Relations said in its report. Land reforms indeed cannot be the gift of a benign government. Experience, however, shows that wherever and whenever there is a sign of the poor peasantry and the deprived and exploited farm workers asserting their rights, the entire power of the established political-administrative order is brought into play to put them down. The administrative and law and order machinery is always found to be on the side of the landed gentry and rich peasants. Legal procedures and niceties are readily cast aside to protect the vested interests. This is in sharp contrast to the extremely judicial and cautious view that is taken in dealing with incidents which implicate the vested interests. Can the Panchayati Raj, as sanctified at last in the Constitution of India change this state of affairs? This is a moot point. But it will be useful and interesting to watch how the poor peasantry and farm workers organise themselves to assert their rights within the Panchayati Raj set-up. The Constitution has certainly given legal sanctions for wider scope and space for the poor peasantry and farm workers to organise and assert their rights; but there will still be pitfalls and conflicts in the way. Any worthwhile progress towards equity in agrarian and social relations in the countryside, indeed the country as a whole, will not be smooth and painless. It will be possible only if the democratic awareness will gather further strength in the Indian polity and society and is not smothered by vested interests under false pretences.

Farm Workers: Erosion of Status

So far as farm workers are concerned, they constituted 9.7 per cent of total agricultural labour households in 1950-51 and increased rapidly to 26.63 per cent because of "change" of erstwhile tenants into "attached labour" in order to thwart laws conferring security of tenure and better terms in share-cropping to tenants. This, in effect, meant reducing the status of tenants to that of bonded labourers or serfs. As for others who escaped this fate and for whom the wage system prevails, the position is equally grim. The minimum wages prescribed for farm workers is still pitifully low and there is evidence to show that there has been sharp erosion of the real value of wages in spite of increases in agricultural production and productivity and improvements in the terms of trade and procurement prices for agricultural produce. The gains of production and productivity in agriculture have, in fact, been monopolised by the landed interests and the rights of agricultural labourer have gone by default. In contrast to this, landed gentry and rich farmers have been pampered and their claims and ambitions have grown.

3

Tryst With Implementing Land Reforms

In India, the land reforms programme has remained one of the major policies for rural development ever since the inception of the planning process. The programme has been designed to break the old feudal socio-economic structure of rural India to provide a greater fillip to agriculture and its productivity. It has also been intended to bring the largest possible number of poor farmers and farm workers in the mainstream of the process of economic development in the country.

As is well-known, possession of a plot of agricultural land, howsoever small, carries with it a high psychological and social value. It helps raise the status of the weaker sections of the society and gives them a sense of belonging to the hub of social life. The land reforms programme has, therefore, been rightly viewed as not only an economic development measure but also as a tool for social uplift.

Objective of Land Reforms

The major objectives of land reforms in India, as identified in the Eighth Plan as well, are as follows:

1. Restructuring of agrarian relations to achieve egalitarian social structure;
2. Elimination of exploitation in land relations;
3. Actualisation of the goal of 'land to the tiller';
4. Improvement of socio-economic conditions of the rural poor by widening their land base;
5. Increasing agricultural production and productivity;
6. Facilitating land base development of the rural poor; and
7. Infusion of a greater measure of equality in local institutions.

Structural Weakness

There is no doubt that Indian rural sector has been suffering from certain structural weaknesses that have obstructed the rural people from availing themselves of the full benefits of liberalisation of the economy. Even today more than 76 per cent of land holdings in India are less than two ha and two-thirds of these holdings are less than one ha. The holdings are fast becoming unoperational and uneconomical. With the reduced size of holdings, more than two-thirds of these farmers are net purchasers of agricultural commodities and even food grains. The sector could not effectively participate in the free market as the holdings are too small to become 'farm firms', a commercially viable proposition.

Revamping Farm Sector: Total Neglect

The reform process in the agricultural sector has been primarily concerned with the role of the market and easing the pressure that agriculture exerts on fiscal deficit, while the need for change in the agrarian structure has conveniently been ignored. For example, much of the traditional thinking on agrarian reforms is based on the principle that ownership is also control. This has blurred the distinction between a dominant landlord who leases out land to control tenants and a small owner who leases out land because he does not have the resources to cultivate. So far, an effective land market has not been created where agricultural land could be freely sold and purchased as well as leased out without fear of losing the right of ownership.

Aside from the socio-political aspects of land reforms, the economic logic is that only when the tiller of the land is made the owner of the soil which he tills, he would develop an incentive to get the best out of the land and try to maximise its yield or returns. The concept of economic size and viability of holdings should be applied to find out whether the beneficiaries of land reforms have adequate access to agricultural inputs like seeds, water, fertilizer and finance and the ability to market their output.

When the tenants are motivated in this manner, the total agricultural output would increase, rural incomes would rise, leading to larger savings and higher levels of investment in the rural economy itself. Surely, a country which depends on the agricultural sector for a substantial part of its national income must improve it for an upsurge in national economic activities. In fact, more than anything else, such a measure would create all-round peace and harmony, cutting across communal barriers, castes and creeds.

Need for a Uniform Land Use Policy

The flip side of the story is that today about 175 million ha of about 329 million ha of the country's land is threatened by various types of land degradation and leading to ever-increasing depletion of productivity. Further, an area of 150 million ha is affected by water or wind erosion. Another 25 million ha area is affected by waterlogging, ravines, alkali and saline soils, shifting cultivation, etc. Further, about 40 million ha are affected by floods and 260 million ha are subject to drought. 'Wanton misuse' has led to the poor health of soil and land resources and an impoverished environment. Besides, frequent and regular floods and droughts in different parts of the country are evidence of improper use of land in the catchments and inadequate conservation and use of rain water. It is, therefore, imperative to have a uniform policy for land use through a uniform land reforms code to be adopted by all the States.

It is estimated that by AD 2000, marginal farms will increase by 33 per cent, while small, semi-medium and large farms will decrease by about 23, 29 and 50 per cent respectively. It is felt that the growing proportion of agricultural labour in the total work-force introduces a greater element of hired labour, thereby further accelerating the capitalistic relations in agricultural operations. Also, injustice has been done to small landowners under the tenancy laws. In some States, they were not allowed to resume land for self-cultivation. Widows and minors had not been given adequate protection. In Nagaland, nobody knows how much land one possessed. There is also no land revenue of any kind and sale/ purchase takes place without the intervention of the community. Land would not be generally sold to another tribe and there is no tenancy of any kind. The land disputes are settled by the tribal council.

Integrating Land Ownership With Productivity

Land reforms have so far been looked at from the standpoint of land ownership, land ceiling and security of tenure. However, for enabling small and marginal fanners to produce more, land reform will have to be given an ownership-cum-production interpretation covering steps which will facilitate the more efficient use of land. For example, without land consolidation and levelling, it becomes difficult to manage water supply and thereby full benefits from our investment on irrigation are not reaped. Hence, land reforms in our country should include steps not only relating to the equitable distribution of available land resource among all sections of the rural community but also measures such as consolidation of holdings, land-levelling and soil-health care which are essential for sustained agricultural productivity. Land ownership and land productivity should both become integral components of the land reform measures.

The slow progress in land reforms is largely attributed to the prevalence of benami land holdings which call for a countrywide movement against this illegal practice. Not only the acquisition and redistribution of surplus land, but even consolidation of holdings has become impossible because of benami lands. The area declared under the land ceiling laws as surplus is less than two per cent of the total cultivated acreage. A large part of this land, too, is held up due to litigation and is not available for distribution.

Against this background, land reforms need an integrated programme of measures meant to eliminate obstacles in socio-economic development that arise out of the defects in the agrarian structure. As such, for deriving maximum benefits from organisation of ownership of tenancy, policy efforts need to be directed towards improving terms of tenancy, reorganisation of availability of credit, providing the various agricultural inputs at reasonable rates, and the marketing facilities with the least inconvenience or any kind of exploitation. Surely, no socio-economic transformation can take place merely by a break-up of large landed properties in our rural sector and/or their redistribution to the landless labourers if there is no improvement in their economic viability.

Marginalisation of the poor: Enforcement of ceiling on land holdings has remained no more edifying than the abolition of intermediary tenures or the implementation of the tenancy reform measures. Even today, only 2.4 per cent landholders are operating 22.3 per cent of the area under cultivation. On the other hand, 74.5 per cent farmers are holding only 26.3 per cent of the area. This fact underscores the skewed pattern of land holdings in India at present. Holdings above 10 ha constituting 2.4 per cent operate as much as 22.87 per cent of the total area. All this signifies marginalisation of the poor peasant and effective concentration of land in a few, despite land ceiling laws. Surveys made recently have revealed that most of the redistributed land has reverted to the original owners.

Non-Implementation of Ceiling Laws

The growing proportion of agricultural labour in the total work-force has introduced a greater element of hired labour, thereby further accentuating the capitalistic relations in agricultural operations. Also, injustice has been done to small landowners under the tenancy laws. Intermediary tenancies have still to be completely abolished. What is worse, where intermediary tenancy has been abolished, concealed tenancies have surfaced with no rights and security for such tenants. The efforts of the State governments to identify such tenants and record them in revenue registers have been dismal as also is the performance of the States in the implementation of the ceiling laws.

The biggest defect is the one pertaining to the permission to obtain land for 'personal cultivation'. The zamindars could even evict tenants for the purpose. 'Personal cultivation' has been defined loosely to include personal supervision by the zamindar or members of his family. Though the official documents claimed that zamindari has been completely abolished, the fact remained that it had only changed its garb. The previous zamindars acquired large areas for personal cultivation for agricultural operations with the help of hired agricultural labour. Yet, however, there is no denying the fact that exploitation and oppression of tenants and actual tillers of the soil declined steeply and the feudal structure crumbled down.

It is true that following the abolition of intermediary tenures like zamindars and jagirdars in most parts of the country, some 20 million tenants had come in direct contract with the State. However, in Andhra Pradesh (Andhra area), Bihar, Haryana, Punjab, Tamil Nadu, West Bengal, Orissa and Assam, ownership rights on tenants have still to be conferred either wholly or partially. While the 'Operation Barga' in West Bengal brought about 1.3 million bargadars (share-croppers) on records, similar attempts have not been made in Bihar or Tamil Nadu and the tenancies in these States are not largely on record. Naturally, therefore, without bringing the tenants and share-croppers on records the security of tenurial rights cannot be ensured and these persons cannot get even a crop loan from credit institutions.

In the context of defective or absence of land records, the Wadhwa Committee appointed by the Planning Commission to evaluate the situation concerning record of rights in land, suggested the establishment of an autonomous statutory corporation called 'Land Title Corporation'. The committee also recommended a change-over from the present system of presumptive titles to land to conclusive titles.

Providing Immunity

Experience so far has shown that land reforms could not be implemented adequately as either the laws were defective or implementation was stalled through litigation. In the matter of ceiling on holdings, the State governments just could not take possession of all the area declared surplus mainly due to litigation. To obviate such difficulties, the Constitution (49th Amendment) Act, 1983 was enacted by Parliament in August 1984. It put 14 land reform laws in the Ninth Schedule of the Constitution providing immunity to these measures from being challenged in a court of law. Again, the Constitution (81st) Amendment Bill, 1994 was passed in 1995 placing land reform laws in seven States under the Ninth Schedule. The States of Bihar, Karnataka, Kerala, Orissa, Rajasthan, Tamil Nadu and West Bengal had sought the inclusion of some of their Acts relating to land reforms in the Ninth Schedule so that they are not challenged in court.

Distributing Surplus Land: The distribution of ceiling surplus land is an important programme under land reforms monitored by the Central government, as land reforms are basic to all rural development programmes aimed at improving the lot of the rural poor. While most of the surplus land available without any dispute has been distributed, a large area is still covered by litigation. States have been advised to take special steps, including setting up of tribunals, to dispose off the pending cases in the High Courts and to speed up the distribution of the remaining ceiling surplus land. There should be a time-bound programme for distribution of ceiling surplus land.

Absence of Proper Land Records

Laws relating to security of tenure could not be implemented effectively due to absence of correct and up-to-date land records. A person could not claim that he was a tenant if his name did not appear in the land records. As a result of laws conferring ownership rights on tenants in various States, about 40 lakh tenants acquired ownership rights over 90 lakh acres. This was much less than the number of tenants who were entitled to purchase ownership rights. Many tenants just could not afford to pay the purchase price while others were unwilling to purchase as landlords pressurised the tenants into submitting that they were not interested.

What is to be taken into account is that without bringing

the tenants and share-croppers on record, security of tenurial rights cannot be ensured and these persons cannot get even a crop loan from credit institutions. In fact, one of the main reasons for inadequate growth in rice production in the eastern region has been the prevalence of share-croppers in Bihar and Orissa which, in turn, has led to inadequate flow of inputs and credit as well as inadequate development of land and exploitation of ground water.

Unfavourable Power Structure

Quite interestingly, while the feudal order has been done away with, the feudal elements emerged stronger and more powerful. As the present elite does not concede any steps that would undermine their economic and political power, any future policy alternative has necessarily to accept the present power structure in our villages. The power structure is heavily in favour of big owners of land who hold numerous position sin public life. In fact, they have also created their vested interests through their own lobby in State Assemblies and Parliament.

The land reform measures become crucial in view of the fact that while the poor at the grass roots level suffered, the affluent at the top lived in splendid isolation. The government having rejected the trickle-down theory of rural and agricultural development, there is a critical need to restructure the land relations in die village comrnunity. As is well-known, the cause of the downtrodden has always gone by default. All this has resulted in a total apathy of the government in the implementation of ceiling laws which have been enacted only to placate the feeling of the gullible farmers and the have-nots. If this state of affairs continues, then the pace of our agricultural progress and economic development of the country would be retarded further.

Need for Special Efforts

Efforts need to be made to bring the informal and oral tenants on record and to provide them security of tenures. Redetermination of ceiling limits, doing away with the exemptions provided for various categories in the laws and a stricter definition of family and personal cultivation are issues which call for urgent action. Special efforts have to be made in the remaining period of the Eighth Plan and in the Ninth Plan period to protect the rights of tenants and sharecroppers, especially in the delineation of the consolidated areas. Correct and up-to-date land records are essential for effective implementation of land reforms.

It is true that land reforms, if implemented seriously, could enrich the content of the programmes for alleviation of poverty. There is ample evidence to show that small farms are cultivated more intensively than large farms. The Green Revolution should now be spread to the eastern States where land redistribution is a major problem. Likewise, there is an utter need for extending the Green Revolution to small fanners all over the country.

Tardy progress despite Plans: In Plan after Plan, the objectives relating to land reforms, the measures required to achieve them and the policy issues involved, including those pertaining to changes in law, have been discussed and delineated in detail but nothing much has really taken off the ground so far. The Sixth Plan, for example, comments that "If the progress of land reforms has been less than satisfactory, it has not been due to flaws in policy but to indifferent implementation." The Plan adds: "the necessary determination has been lacking due to ineffectively undertaken action, particularly in the matter of implementation of ceiling laws, consolidation of holdings and in not vigorously pursuing concealed tenancies and having them vested with tenancy occupancy rights as enjoined under the law." The same tenor of helplessness is evident in the subsequent Plans.

Protecting Degraded Land: Soon, in the face of the population explosion taking place in the country, which may raise the population to about one billion requiring 240 million tonnes of food grains by the end of this century, the need to control soil erosion and land degradation, besides restoring the health of the already degraded land, assumes great importance. For, no amount of investment in fertilizers, irrigation and other inputs can help in achieving the desired target of about six million tonnes increase in food grains production every year, if the health of the basic inelastic resource is not adequately protected.

According to the available statistics, the per capita availability of land in the country is 0.5 ha, which is likely to decrease to 0.33 ha by the end of the century. Similarly, the per capita land available for cultivation will decline from the present 0.2 ha to 0.14 ha. On the other hand, an additional 60 million ha will be required to meet the demands for food, fodder and firewood and about 12 million ha for human settlements, roads, railways, industries, etc.

In sum, land reforms do not involve only redistribution of land as is commonly believed. It also involves issues like whose land is being redistributed, what type of land is there for the purpose, what is the objective of redistribution, etc. In many cases, formal take-over of land by the States has not been allowed by its demarcation into plots. There are instances of blocks of land having been allocated to a number of assignees without demarcating the share of each. Deeds of assignments do not clearly state which part of land has been assigned. No steps have been taken for recording the rights of the assignees in the record of rights or other relevant documents.

Ushering in Growth & Social Justice

It is necessary to thoroughly reform the existing system and to plug the loopholes that perpetrate down the village level. Let us remember that a redistribution of five per cent of the cultivated area from holdings above five acres to small farmers and agricultural labour will have the effect of increasing incomes accruing to them by about 20 per cent. Hence, land reform measures must be accorded the highest priority in our scheme of things for economic development. Land reform legislation so far enacted can only be said to be the foundation for the measures that are yet to be taken up.

It is also true that in spite of non-implementation, defective implementation or non-existence of certain land reform measures, agricultural production has been increasing. However, if more supplementary measures of positive help to the vast majority of farmers through legislation or otherwise, along with plugging the existing loopholes in the present laws, are adopted, a new era of quantum jump in agricultural progress could be heralded soon.

Therefore, new measures should bring about economic efficiency and social justice. As a result of adoption of land reform measures so far, the current features of the Indian agrarian economy reveal the existence of three distinct sectors of Indian agriculture, coexisting and contending with one another. The first is the developed sector of modern entrepreneur farmers who are rich. The second one comprises the area under self-cultivation by medium, small and marginal farmers. The third sector is consisted of the vast area of land under utilisation by share-croppers and various kinds of tenants and subtenants having no proprietary rights in land, no security of tenure, no share in the various aids and inputs distributed by the State or institutional agencies. It is this third sector which is the worst placed in the agrarian economy and is still subject to various forms of semi-feudal exploitation such as rack-renting, usury, economic bondage and caste and social oppression.

Concluding Observations

The principal components of an effective land reform strategy seem to be: *(a)* political commitment at the top, *(b)* administrative preparedness, including the improvement of the technical design of enactments, the provision of financial resources and the streamlining of the organisational machinery of implementation, *(c)* creation of necessary supporting services for the beneficiaries, and *(d)* the organisation of beneficiaries themselves. Tenancy reforms should be directed to the stage of finally breaking up the landlord-tenant nexus. Agriculture should be treated as a family occupation of the peasant-cultivator and not as a source of subsidiary unearned income. In a normal peasant-proprietor system, there is no place for absentee landlordism which should be discouraged and ultimately curbed.

The ceiling laws enacted by different States are designed to make a dent on the concentration of land ownership. It is necessary that these laws are enforced effectively and speedily. Firm measures are required against fictitious and benami transfers deliberately effected by big landowners to circumvent ceiling laws. It can be said that apart from fixing a ceiling, a floor level may also be decided but it may not be feasible to do so in view of the unemployment situation in the country. For people living below the poverty line, land, howsoever small it may be, is the only source of livelihood at present.

Finally, land reforms cannot be properly enforced without popular co-operation and support at all levels. Popular supervisory committees should, therefore, be constituted at all levels, consisting of people's representatives, including beneficiaries, officials and experts to exercise vigilance on implementation. These committees may be vested with certain statutory powers like that of inspection of records and sites, collection of evidence and so on. Their recommendations and suggestions should receive due weightage and full acceptance by the government.

It is also important that potential beneficiaries are made aware of the land reforms programme. The existing socio-economic order in which the power base lies with the rural rich needs to be radically changed to a new order in which power balance will favour the rural poor. The recent developments in regard to biotechnology in agriculture have made the small-peasant agriculture potentially viable. Likewise, new institutional innovations in the field of research, price support, credit supply, water management and other inputs are going to have immense impact on the totality of Indian agrarian structure. In the ultimate analysis, land reforms would improve the future prospects in relation to raising farm productivity, income and employment through the creation of new incentives and opportunities for increased work and investment.

Land Reforms: Issues and Challenges

A major concern of planning in India has been the development of rural areas and rural people. Rural development implies both the economic betterment of people as well as greater social transformation. Development has to be participatory with people having the opportunity to enhance their capabilities. People's participation in the developmental process would ensure its sustainability. Apart from increased participation of people in the rural development process, decentralization of planning, better enforcement of land reforms, and greater access to credit and inputs would go a long way in providing better prospects for economic development of the rural people.

Thus, redistributive land reforms become a vital instrument for alleviation of poverty and increasing productivity in agriculture as well. Although, most of the States have enacted legislation providing for security of tenure to the tenants, yet oral and informal tenancies with cultivating possession still exist without being brought on record in many areas of the country under the guise of "personal cultivation".

In fact, land reforms is a part of heritage of our national freedom movement. The poverty in our rural society and extreme exploitation of peasantry by intermediaries, moneylenders, and others, leading to their impoverishment and misery attracted the attention of national leaders during the freedom struggle. The comprehensive and reforms policy which thus evolved consisted of:

(a) abolition of intermediaries and bringing of tenants in direct contact with the State;
(b) tenancy reforms to provide security to actual cultivators of land against eviction;
(c) redistribution of land by. imposition of ceiling on agriculture holdings;
(d) consolidation of holdings; and
(e) updating of land records.

Abolition of Intermediaries

Abolition of intermediary tenure during 1950-55, essentially involved removal of the intermediary levels or layers of interests in land between the State and the actual cultivators, bringing the actual cultivator in direct relationship with the State, giving permanent rights in land to them and rationalisation of the land revenue system. However, the original objective was diluted as some States took unduly long to bring the law on the statute-books. Even after it came into existence, its implementation was blocked by erstwhile landlords through prolonged legal battles. After the abolition of intermediaries and taking over of State, surveys and settlement of land have yet to be completed in many States. Further, under the law intermediaries were allowed to take with them a huge area of land under the garb of 'personal cultivation'. These lands continued to be operated by tenants and share-croppers who got no protection from these measures.

Tenancy Reforms

The tenancy reform measures were built around: *(a)* rent payable to the landowner not to exceed one-fifth to one-fourth of gross produce; *(b)* tenants be given permanent right to the land they cultivate subject to a limited right of resumption to be given to landowners; and *(c)* landlord-tenant relationship be ended by conferring ownership rights on tenants in respect of non-resumable land.

Tenancy legislation were enacted by States incorporating some or all of the above features. However, tenancy reform does not seem to have made much impact, if the position is to be judged by the incidence of informal or oral tenancies today. Such tenancies have come up even where leasing has been expressly banned. Thus, providing some modicum of security to this category of tenants is the most burning problem of agrarian reform today which has persisted from British times despite more than four decades of land reform implementation.

Land Ceiling

Fixation of ceiling on agricultural holdings was taken up predominantly as a redistribute measure. The compelling case of land ceiling arose from the absolute and permanent shortage of land. The idea basically was to ration land, a crucial asset, in such a way that, above a certain maximum, the surplus land is taken away from the present holders and is distributed to the landless or small holders in accordance with certain priorities. The skewed distribution of land in India with nearly a quarter of the rural households owning no land at all and another one-fifth owning less than an acre each provided ample social and economic reasons for the use of ceiling as a means of redressing this imbalance. The ceiling question gave rise to more debate and arguments than any other reform issue as it touched on the raw nerve of tampering with private property rights. Legislation for ceiling on the existing holdings and future acquisition were enacted in most States during the Second Plan period. The policy with reference to the enactment and implementation of ceiling legislation differed among the States. The ceiling limits were different because of different types of land and their income-giving capacity. There were also differences in the law on some other aspects. To bring about some degree of uniformity, the ceiling laws were revised on the basis of national guidelines evolved in 1972. Some States, however, have lower ceiling than those recommended in these guidelines. Judged by the quantum of land declared surplus, this reform measure has not achieved the desired objective fully. The provision of large number of exemptions from ceilings and many loopholes in the legislation led to frequent interventions by courts of law. The malafide transfers reduced the quantum of surplus land.

Bhoodan Movement: Quite independent of the ceiling legislation, almost preceding it, another attempt at redistribution of land was made through the Bhoodan (landgift) movement. Through this movement, Vinoba Bhave impressed upon the landowners to demonstrate their compassion by donating one-sixth of their holdings and envisaged that the land so collected would then be suitably redistributed. This movement, however, failed to have any appreciable impact on the problem of landlessness and inequitous distribution.

Consolidation of Land Holdings

Consolidation of fragmented land holdings though necessary for efficiency and economy in agriculture and better development planning at the village level is not essentially a redistributive measure. It is simply a rearrangement of land on the basis of existing rights. Even so, most States have not shown any enthusiasm for it. Some have either relegated it to a 'voluntary' character or have not enacted any law for it or have kept the already enacted law in abeyance. Apart from increasing pressure on land and lack of alternative employment opportunities outside the farm sector inhibiting the progress of this programme, consolidation operations are generally feared to favour the more influential and substantial land owners. The small land owners, therefore, feel that they would not get a fair deal. Besides, experience has been that sub-tenants and share-croppers with no recorded evidence of their rights get evicted through this process.

Consolidation of fragmented land holdings has already achieved a fair degree of success in increasing agricultural production resolving land-based conflicts and bringing better harmony and social facilities to village life in those parts of the country which are serviced by canal irrigation. In other parts of the country, it has not made much headway because of the feeling of insecurity among the small and marginal farmers, share-croppers and tenants on account of their apprehension that they may get an unfair deal. This sense of insecurity among the weaker sections could be allayed if prior to taking up consolidation, land reform measures pertaining to security of tenure etc are effectively implemented. Since consolidation of land holdings is considered necessary for overcoming the obstacles which come in the way of intensive cultivation and permanent improvement of land, it needs to be taken up on a priority basis in areas covered by stable irrigation system preceded by recording of tenants and share-croppers and updating of land records.

Land Records: It is an admitted fact that in most States land records are not up-to-date and even where land records are regularly rewritten, the ground level reality is not reflected in them, particularly regarding tenancy and share-cropping. This has been largely due to pressures from landowning classes with the specific objective of subverting legal provisions regarding protection to tenants and sharecroppers. The State governments have been usually responsive to such pressures.

Plight of Tenants

Despite the lack of desired success in achieving the objective set out for the comprehensive land reform policy, land reforms as an issue is not likely to just fade away. This is because land is central to village economy and about 80 per cent of rural people depend upon land for their survival. A large number of these people are either landless agricultural labourers or/and tenants and share-croppers working on oral leases which make them liable to eviction. Rents in most parts are commonly 50 or 60 per cent of the crop even when the landlord contributes only the land while all other factors of production are supplied by the tenants. In this situation of insecurity of tenure with high rents, neither any surplus is left with the cultivator to invest in land nor there is any incentive to put in more labour since the greater beneficiary of such an effort would be the landowner. Besides, in many cases, the margin of subsistence is so narrow that tenants can afford little risk; any innovation in productive practices that goes wrong may result in starvation. Apart from these crippling conditions, credit facilities are not available to such share-croppers in the absence of any evidence of their status in the record of rights. For this very reason, even the benefits of the law regarding security of tenure do not accrue to them.

Land: A Powerful Tool

Land reforms have largely been looked upon as a part of rural development activities because restructuring of agrarian relation is considered necessary for improving agricultural production and productivity. It is not sufficiently realised that in our rural society, land is important not merely as a factor of production but it provides a social status to its holder. Even a small piece of land restores to the rural poor human dignity and helps them in disengaging themselves from the exploitative relationship imposed by the landowners. Land reforms, therefore, have in this context more than a mere economic rationale. They contribute to redistribution of social status and political power and help in establishment of a more egalitarian society. A more egalitarian social order would naturally permit the rural poor, the deprived and the weak to absorb benefits of various development programmes which may otherwise be cornered by the more powerful who socially and economically control the rural poor. In this sense also, effective implementation of land reforms cannot be avoided.

4

Land Reforms in Tribal Areas

After about half a century of Independence, during which time almost all the States and Union Territories came to have laws and regulations to prevent alienation of tribal land to non-tribals and to restore the lands alienated over specified periods of time, tribal land alienation continues to be an issue of common concern. Among politicians and emotionally attached anthropologists, it has indeed become a folklore. Reality, however, is quite different from such perceptions, and from what it may have been decades ago. Besides the protection and restoration measures, a number of developments have taken place which have changed the scenario for the better. Special programmes of tribal development under Five Year Plans, increasing integration of tribal economies into the market system, penetration of market forces into the economic basis of the tribal communities, leading to economic differentiation within them, rise of political consciousness crystallising into violent and non-violent tribal movements for self-protection (ethnic identity), for autonomy, for separate State formation, and even for secession in some cases of the North-East, have all contributed to the changed scenario. An important underlying factor that has also played a role is the increasing pressure of tribal population itself on tribal lands, as reflected in the relatively higher growth rate of tribal population compared to the general population of the country (Table-l).

Since historically the pressure of non-tribal population on tribal lands has not been uniform in all the regions of Ideal concentration, the problem of alienation is best considered in the regional historical perspective. A brief account of that perspective is provided in subsequent lines. Whereas land laws and regulations have cared for alienation of tribal lands to non-tribal, for a number of reasons, the scope of alienation has widened to include State demand on tribal lands and private demand on tribal community land. It is, therefore, necessary to have a comprehensive view of tribal land alienation process. Such a view is presented in a separate section. The incidence or the extent of land alienation at all-India level and in the regions of tribal concentration has been discussed subsequently. Our conclusions are given in the last section.

Regional Historical Perspective

The tribal population of the country (68 million according to 1991 census) is found in three gional re-concentrations: the Central Indian belt, the North-East and the Peninsular South. The Central Indian belt, stretching from sea-to-sea on the east-west axis, edging on the Ganga-Yamuna plains to the north, bound by the Godavari to the South, separated from the Thar desert by the Aravalis, and spanned by the Vindhya and Satpura ranges with plains, plateaus and river valleys scattered all around, accounts for as large as 83 per cent of the country's tribal population. This region has been like a frontier land of the country, where immigrants have been moving since ancient times. During the medieval and the modern colonial period the native States and the colonial government encouraged non-tribal peasants to settle in the region with a view to maximize land revenue (Kosambi, 1956; S.N. Mishra, 1989; Janardan

Rao, 1987). In the post-Independence period this region has become the hub of India's upcoming industrial civilisation endowed as it is with all sorts of minerals, metals and coal reserves. As a concomitant, non-tribals have been moving in along with industrial and mining development projects. Furthermore, the projects themselves have been putting up additional demand for land resulting in tribal land alienation to the State.

In contrast to the Central Indian region, areas of tribal concentration in the North-East, which accounts for 12 per cent of the country's population, has virtually remained a cul-de-sac until after Independence when State agencies began moving in with modern development plans. And, the partition of the country created an exceptional situation in Tripura where non-tribal settlers from East Bengal overwhelmed the tribal population of the State. The inaccessibility of tribal areas in the North-East to non-tribal was formalised when the British introduced the 'Inner Line Regulation' late last century. That Regulation is still in force in the States of Arunachal Pradesh, Nagaland and Mizoram. Whatever non-tribal is there in the tribal majority States is almost wholly urban, having little to do with land and lane cultivation, or for that matter with alienation of tribal land to non-tribal. However, there is another type of land alienation that has been taking place in these States, namely alienation of common community lands into private hands. As a result of programmes of converting land under shifting cultivation to permanent cultivation and horticulture, there is aggressive urge to acquire private property in land at the expense of community lands (S.N. Mishra, 1985, 1987).

The third region of tribal concentration, the Peninsular South, along the Eastern and Western Ghats and the Nilgiri Hills accounts for four per cent of the country's tribal population. Historically, few if any of the region's tribes had developed to the stage of settled agriculture. While some had reached the stage of shifting agriculture, most

Table 1: Regional Growth Pattern of Tribal Population in India, 1971-91

Regions	*Population (lakhs)*			*Per cent to total*			*Annual growth Rate (Per cent)*	
	1971	1981	1991	1971	1981	1991	1971-81	1981-91
I. Central Indian Belt	354.56	448.76	561.33	86.16	90.06	82.84	2.65	2.50
1. Andhra Pradesh	22.26	31.76	42.00				4.27	3.22
2. Bihar	49.33	58.11	66.17				1.78	1.38
3. Gujarat	37.57	48.49	61.62				2.91	2.70
4. M.P.	98.15	119.87	153.99				2.21	2.84
5. Maharashtra	34.41	57.72	73.18				1.62	2.67
6. Orissa	59.15	70.32	1.66				1.88	
7. Rajasthan	31.35	41.83	54.75				3.34	3.00
8. W.B.	26.03	30.71	38.09				1.80	2.40
9. Goa, Damman, Diu	0.07	0.11	0.12				5.71	0.99
10. Dadra & Nagar Haveli	0.64	0.82	1.09				2.81	3.29
II. Peninsular South And Oceanic Group	9.53	8.41	28.86	2.32	1.69	4.25	2.17	1.53
11. Karnataka	2.62	—	19.16				—	—
12. Kerala	1.93	2.61	3.21				3.51	2.29
13. Tamil Nadu	4.50	5.20	5.74				1.56	1.03

14. Andaman & Nicobar Island	0.18	0.22	0.27				2.22	2.27
15. Lakshadweep	0.30	0.38	0.48				2.67	2.63
III. North West Himalayas	3.41	4.30	5.06	0.83	0.87	0.75	2.61	1.76
16. H.P.	1.40	1.97	2.18				3.87	1.06
17. U.P.	1.99	2.33	2.88				1.71	2.35
IV. North-East India	43.98	36.76	82.33	10.69	7.38	12.15	3.17	4.57
18. Assam	16.07	28.74	6.28					
19. Manipur	3.34	3.88	6.32				1.62	4.10
20. Meghalaya	8.14	10.76	15.18				3.26	6.28
21. Nagaland	4.58	6.51	10.61				4.21	4.10
22. Sikkim	0.52	0.75	0.91				4.23	6.29
23. Tripura	4.51	5.84	8.53				2.95	2.13
24. Arunachal Pradesh	3.69	4.41	5.50				4.76	4.60
25. Mizoram	3.13	4.62	6.54				4.15	
India (Total) Excluding Assam & Karnataka	411.48	677.58	392.79	498.04	629.68		2.51	2.64

Source: Census of India (Series 1) 1971, 1981, 1991.

Note: Data for Assam and Karnataka for the year 1981 are 28.74, 18.25 lakhs respectively, which is absurdly high.

had lived by foodgathering, hunting, fishing and collection of forest produce. In the post-Independence period effort has been made under the tribal development plans to transform the tribes into settled cultivators by allotment of lands at the peripheries of their forest habitat, and by providing other kinds of required support. At best the effort has produced mixed results (P.K. Mishra, 1982). Several of the tribes with their forest-dwelling culture did not have the motivation nor could develop the skill of settled cultivation. The result is that their land has been alienated to their better observation of Chenchu rehabilitation settlement called Bairluti at the foot of the Eastern Ghat, on the road from Chenchus of the settlement had either sold out, mortgaged or given their land to the Lambada tribals on rent at the time of my visit in 1983.

Thus, we see that the three regions of tribal concentration because of differences of history, geographical location,

Table 2: Percentage of Tribal and Non-Tribal Households Reporting Disposal of Land by State/UT

SL.No.	*State/UT/Region*	*%age of Households reporting disposal of land*		*No. of sample reporting disposal of land*	
		Tribal	*Non-Tribal*	*Tribal*	*Non-Tribal*
1.	Andhra Pradesh	0.8	3.8	8	35
2.	Bihar	1.3	6.1	20	41
3.	Gujarat	1.3	0.6	17	5
4	Madhya Pradesh	0.5	2.5	14	31
5.	Maharashtra	1.0	4.2	13	35
6.	Orissa	2.3	9.3	27	59
7.	Rajasthan	1.0	1.7	6	12
8.	West Bengal	4.7	9.8	34	62
9.	Dadra & Nagar Haveli	0.8	—	2	0
10.	Central Tribal belt	1.7		4.9	
11.	Arunachal Pradesh	2.0	—	9	0
12.	Assam	1.3	1.2	7	4

13.	Meghalaya	1.7	7.1	6	3
14.	Mizoram	0.2	—	1	0
15.	Sikkim	0.2	0.6	1	2
16.	Tripura	1.3	0.1	5	1
17.	North-East Region	1.4		1.2	
18.	Himachal Pradesh	1.7	3.6	3	7
19.	Karnataka	—	1.7	0	11
20.	Kerala	5.3	8.7	8	35
21.	Tamil Nadu	4.8	3.6	4	16
22.	Uttar Pradesh	3.9	4.3	6	7
23.	Andaman & Nicobar Is	—	—	0	0
24.	Lakshadweep	3.0	2.4	3	1
25.	Other State/U.T.	2.9		3.5	
26	All-India	1.4	4.4	194	367

Source: NSSO, Report No. 380, Statement (14) Department of Statistics, Government of India, 1991.

stage of development along the ladder from total dependence on forest for food to food production by practice of settled cultivation present very different picture in respect of actual or potential alienation of tribal lands. Whereas the Central Indian region has been the main theatre of tribal land alienation to non-tribals, except for Tripura the North-East has been closed to such alienation, and remains as such. In the Peninsular South, tribal land alienation is largely a post-Independence phenomenon.

Land Alienation Process

In its simplest form and as a one shot affair, land alienation is disposal of land by formal or informal sale, gift or transfer for a price or compensation. Since protective laws prohibit sale or transfer of tribal land to non-tribal, if it takes place, it takes place formally to other tribal and informally to non-tribal. Rather than this form of simple transaction, usually the process of land alienation follows a circuitous route. It begins by an advance of consumption loan to a tribal household, followed by further advance, accumulation of debt, failure to repay the debt, and finally mortgage of land against the debt. Failure to redeem the mortgage results into sale or permanent transfer. Usufruct mortgage of land for a loan if unredeemed produces the same result. Leasing-out of land to a non-tribal household, if not resumed for self-cultivation or any other use over a long period of time may turn into perpetual lease amounting to permanent possession of the lessee, although, ordinarily leasing out of land is not covered under land alienation, since the lessor retains the ownership rights. Besides these economic processes of land alienation, extra-economic methods of encroachment on tribal land of its forcible occupation also amount to land alienation.

As we alluded to in the preceding section, acquisition of tribal land by the State for purposes of development projects is another form. of tribal land alienation that has entered the scene in the post-Independence period, even though its incidence may be relatively small. In the North-East, specifically dus to change over to permanent settled cultivation, common community lands are transferred to private possession and ownership of the tribal households, with or without common consent of the villagers. Whereas in the case of State acquisition of tribal land, there is compensation for the land alienated, in the North-Eastern case, there is no evidence that the tribal village community is compensated for its alienated lands (Mishra, 1987).

Until the late 1980s, available studies on tribal land alienation were done by individual scholars and Tribal Research Institutes at micro level tor specific tribes. For the first time, a countrywide survey on the incidence and mode of tribal land alienation was, inter alia, done by the National Sample Survey Organisation (NSSO) in its 44th Round, July 1988-June 1989. The author had played some role in the designing of the survey by submitting a note in a manner suitable to the preparation of the questionnaire schedules, on the request of the then

Chairman of the NSSO, Prof. B.S. Minhas. Limitations of the space do not permit me to go into the survey details. The schedules on Tribal Survey' covered 1,128 villages in districts and blocks of tribal concentration in the country. The stratified sample of households was so chosen as to make it representative. The result of the survey on tribal land alienation are now available in the NSSO Report No. 380 (1991). In the following section, our discussion is based on these survey results.

Incidence of Tribal Land Alienation

The results of the Survey are given in the Table 2. The tribal and non-tribal respondents belonging to the rural sample households in the areas of tribal concentration of the States and Union Territories were asked whether they had disposed of (alienated) land during the last five years; to whom they had disposed and what was the mode of disposal? The persons and agencies to whom disposed were specified as: own tribal, other tribal, non-tribal, government agency, private agency and others. Similarly, modes of disposal were specified as: sale, gift, transfer to settle debt, acquisition by government/public bodies, unauthorised occupation and others. Answer to many more details, for instance, area alienated, were also sought. However, since the number of households reporting disposal being very small, the data have not been tabulated according to those details and characteristics (NSSO, Report No. 380, pp. 58-61). All we have is the percentage of households reporting disposal of land during the last five years, and limited information on persons/agencies to whom the land had been disposed (Report No. 380, Statement 15, p. 61).

It is clear from the Table 2 that tribal land alienation in the country during the mid-1980s was almost negligible. At the all-India level the proportion of tribal households reporting disposal of land was no more than 1.4 per cent of the total. Small in itself, this proportion is smaller even compared to 4.4 per cent of non-tribal households who reported disposal of land. There is no significant difference in the incidence of alienation as between the Central Indian belt and the North-East region. Whereas the proportion of tribal households reporting disposal in the Central tribal belt was 1.7 per cent, in the North-East it was 1.4 per cent. Across States and Union Territories, the maximum reported was five per cent or close to five per cent from Kerala, Tamil Nadu and West Bengal. Notably, Kerala and Tamil Nadu belong to the Peninsular South region of tribal concentration in the country.

The NSSO Report gives information on persons/ agencies to whom land was alienated by the tribal and non-tribal households at the all-India level and for a few States. This is given in Table 3. The reader will notice that of the 1.4 per cent of tribal households reporting land disposal at the all-India level, only 13 per cent disposed it to non-tribal. A majority of tribal (58%) disposed of land to tribal themselves, the remaining 28 per cent disposed it to 'others' which is inclusive of government and other agencies as well. What is equally, and perhaps more interesting is the fact that in the areas of tribal concentration relatively more non-tribal (4.4 per cent) disposed of land and among those who did, as many as 78 per cent disposed it to tribals. Thus, in the areas of tribal concentration in the country, if at all there was land alienation, most of it was in favour of tribals during mid-1980.

Table 3: Number of Households Disposing Land to Various Agencies per 1000 Household Reporting Disposal of Land

Sl. No.	State/UT	Household group	% of reporting disposal of land	Agency to which disposed of				No. of sample households
				Tribal	Non-Tribal	Others	Total	
1.	Andhra Pradesh	Non-Tribal	3.8	665	76	259	1000	35
2.	Bihar	Tribal	1.3	121	67	812	1000	20
		Non-Tribal	6.1	787	104	109	1000	41
3.	Kerala	Non-Tribal	8.7	907	29	64	1000	35
4.	Madhya Pradesh	Non-Tribal	2.5	997 733	3	-	1000 1000	31
	Maharashtra							
5.	Maharashtra	Non-Tribal	4.2	733	143	159	1000	35
6.	Orissa	Tribal	2.3	729	77	194	1000	27
		Non-Tribal	9.3	789	115		1000	59
7.	West Bengal	Tribal Non-Tribal	4.7 9.8	822 758	107 71	71 171	1000 1000	34 62
8.	All-India	Tribal	1.4	583	134	281	1000	194
		Non-Tribal	4.4	776	95	138	1000	367

Source: NSSO, Report No. 380, Statement (IS), Department of Statistics, Government of India, 1991.

Conclusion

The issue of tribal land alienation has been one of persistent concern among planners, policy-makers and to some extent among the intelligentsia. There is no doubt that historically the Central Indian tribal belt has been a region of non-tribal immigration and settlement. In course of time this led to alienation of tribal lands to non-tribal in this region. In the post-Independence period, protective laws and regulations, special programmes of tribal development, and not in the least rise of political consciousness and its crystallization into tribal movements for self-protection, all have combined to change the scenario in respect of tribal land alienation. By the middle of 1980s its incidence had become negligible. More importantly, if at all there was land alienation, it was mostly from non-tribal to tribal in the areas of tribal concentration in the country. Clearly, tribal communities in these areas has succeeded in developing and consolidating their power and position. It is time the commonly held belief that tribal land alienation is endemic as well as widespread be given up.

5

Land Reforms and Distributive Justice: An Empirical Perspective

Rarely does a study on Indian economics open its chapter on agriculture without making a drastic criticism of Indian agrarian structure, and rarely does it end without some proposal or other on land reforms. Land reform proposals occupied the pride of place in the economic programme of Indian National Congress as early as in the beginning of the present century. Credit must go to Gandhiji this the peasant movement became an integral part of the national movement became an integral part of the national movement for Independence. The agitation for political independence became, therefore, not a mere expression of national sentiments, but the manifestation of the urge for reforming the socio-economic structure to eliminate injustice and inequality and give a better deal to the poor rural masses.

After the attainment of Independence, the evils of the tenancy system and absentee landlordism were repeatedly pointed out, the virtues of peasant proprietorship were extolled and the suggestion of co-operative farming was put forth as the solution for the problem of uneconomic holdings. It is against this background this any aspect of land reform in India will have to be examined. The slogan of "Land to the Tillers", implies the surrender of land which one cannot personally—with his own and family—cultivate.

After Independence, the Indian National Congress through its various committees stressed the need for ceiling on landholding to avoid social injustice. The whole idea revolved round the assumption that supply of land in relation to the cultivation was so limited and that the present technique of activation, managerial skills and financial resources were such that the optimum size ought to be fairly low.

The principles of distributive justice appear to be the wash argument in favour of imposing a ceiling on landholdings Further the 'Directive Principles of State Policy' which provide inspiration to economic planning in India, call upon the State to promote the welfare of the people by creating a social order in which justice—social, economic and political—will prevail.

Thus the emphasis on reduction of inequality and promotion of distributive justice is obvious and its influence on Indian planning is natural and inevitable. It can be rightly suggested this the objectives of land policy form the social aspect which is not less important than the economic. A policy for land may be considered adequate in the measures to be taken by government in which, now and in the coming years, it reduces disparities in all respects and finally promises equality of status and opportunity to different sections of the rural masses. The land policy under the Five Year Plans, besides emphasizing distributive aspect of justice, does stress the economic efficiency aspect also.

A careful observation of the objective of land reform speaks of two factors: First, to remove such impediments upon agricultural production as arise from the character of the agrarian structure, and secondly, to create conditions for evolving as speedily as may be possible an agrarian economy with high levels of efficiency and productivity.

Keeping these facts in view the land ceiling Acts of different States provide for acquisition of surplus land by the government and redistributing it among the landless agricultural labours. The basic objective behind this is to alleviate poverty in rural India. However, the results on these fronts have been far from satisfactory basically because of the fact that State governments have not been in a position to implement land reform policies as effectively as it was desired. In this background, the present study is a hin sble attempt to analyse the micro scenario of three States—Haryana, Karnataka and West Bengal. After obtaining the micro view of the prevailing socio-economic condition of assignees of surplus ceiling land the study suggests some legislative and administrative measures which may help accelerate speedy implementation of land reforms.

Relevance of the Study

The relevance of the prt ent study lies in the fact that surrendering of surplus land by the big farmers and land acquired under the Bhoodan movement as also the unused government land has a direct bearing on the land reform policies of the Government of India in general and State governments in particular. Further, it has been noticed that hundreds and thousands acres of land have been acquired by the State governments under the Ceiling Act (both actual acquisition and acquisition on paper only). But either the surplus land has not yet been distributed or distributed, if at all, in a haphazard manner. Again, it has been noticed that if the land has been distributed among the landless, in course of time, they have been dispossessed of land either under economic pressure or by force, both social and political. Similarly, in certain

States it has been noticed that the surplus land has been distributed among such beneficiaries who had their own parental land and were engaged in cultivation. As such, it is in the fitness of things that some study should be conducted to bring to light the factors which help or hinder in improving the socio-economic condition of the rural landless by assigning them the surplus ceiling land.

The usefulness of the study lies in the fact that the conclusions arrived at and suggestions made may help the government to recast its land reform policies and to adopt a new strategy of planning and implementation of land reform policies. As regards the nature of the study it is specific rather than general.

The paper is an abridged form of a major study conducted by the author to assess the socio-economic condition of the assignees of surplus ceiling land in two districts each, i.e. Bhiwani and Narnaul, Mysore and Tumkur and Murshidabad and Nodia, respectively of the States of Haryana, Karnataka and West Bengal. The study was commissioned by the Ministry of Rural Development, Government of India and the findings and recommendations of the study are based on the empirical survey and interview with the beneficiaries of the States concerned.

Objectives

The major objectives of the study were as follows:

i) To examine the criteria of assigning the land to the landless;

ii) To ascertain whether the assignees cultivate the land or have been dispossessed of it;

iii) If dispossessed of land, to ascertain whether it was a result of social and political forces or economic necessities;

iv) If the beneficiaries are cultivating the land, what financial assistance they get from government and other financing agencies;

v) To examine the effectiveness of Land Reform Act in protecting the beneficiaries from dispossession and exploitation;

vi) Based on time-scheduled data, to assess their socio-economic condition after becoming the surplus lane beneficiaries;

vii) To compare and contrast their economic condition with those who have not been benefited from surplus ceiling land;

viii) To locate the bottlenecks which exist in proper implementation of land reform and judicious distribution of surplus ceiling land; and

ix) Finally, based on empirical enquiry, to suggest ways and means for effective and better utilisation of assigned land by the beneficiaries.

Findings and Fulfilment of the Objectives

On the basis of our findings in regard to economic condition of assignees of ceiling land in the three States concerned, i.e. Haryana, Karnataka, and West Bengal, the objectives of the study so designed and their fulfilment could be summarised as follows:

In regard to the first objective, i.e. 'criteria for assigning the land to the landless', there is a common and uniform guideline to be followed in the whole of the country. The following categories of people are entitled to get surplus ceiling land assigned in their names:

(i) Dispossessed tenants who are not registered as occupants;

(ii) Displaced tenants having no land;

(iii) Landless agricultural labourers;

(iv) Landless persons and ex-military personnel whose gross annual income does not exceed Rs. 2,000;

(v) Released bonded labourers; and

(vi) Other persons residing in villages in the same Panchayat and whose gross annual income does not exceed Rs. 2,000.

By and large, in all the three States the above criteria were followed. However, in some cases either due to political pressure or some sort of favouritism a negligible percentage of people who do not fall in the above category got the land assigned in their names. But, such type of cases were reported in greater number in Haryana in comparison to Karnataka and West Bengal. When asked about such irregularities the officials reported that they honestly tried their best to follow the criteria strictly, but undue political interference compelled them to deviate from the set principles. In West Bengal, the criteria used to be followed strictly but due to political Pressure some favours were reported to have been shown to those beneficiaries who were committed to the political ideology of the ruling party, and, naturally some innocent and non-committed genuine beneficiaries are denied the opportunity. In Haryana, a few cases came to our notice in which persons belonging to different villages and different Panchayats had been allotted surplus, ceiling land in distant Panchayat areas, which were against and in violation of the set principles. But, they were insignificant in number.

On the whole, it could be said that by and large, the first objective of the study was achieved in the sense, that the officials tried to adhere, as far as possible, to the guidelines fixed for allotment of surplus ceiling land.

Coming to the second objective, it is heartening to note that, if given the actual possession of the land, beneficiaries generally cultivated the land. This was uniformly, by and large, noticed in all the three States under study. But, this objective may not be said to be fulfilled in the sense that in certain cases in all the three States the actual possession was not given to beneficiaries and as such, the question of cultivating the land by beneficiaries did not arise. The reason for not giving the actual possession of the land was litigation on the said plot as reported by officials.

Only in rare cases the incidence of dispossession was reported by the beneficiaries. In West Bengal, even after giving actual possession of the land in some cases, beneficiaries did not cultivate the land and the reason assigned by them was that the land was so small, and there was such a dearth of facility of irrigation that they could not cultivate on the assigned land. Again, in West Bengal it was reported by a number of beneficiaries that some of the beneficiaries of surplus ceiling land had let out the assigned land to share-croppers which was against and in violation of the rule. Such cases were reported to the government officials by the Research Team during its field visit. In Haryana, it also came to the notice of the Research Team that some beneficiaries had sold their assigned land to the small and big farmers and out of that sale proceeds they had started some business. In some cases, land was assigned to those who were genuine beneficiaries, but were not interested in cultivation.

In regard to the third objective, i.e. 'if dispossessed of land, to ascertain, whether it was a result of social and political forces or economic necessities', it could be said that, if at all there was any dispossession, it was the result of both social and political pressure and economic necessity. However, dispossession on account of economic necessities was negligible as per our observations and findings.

The fifth objective was 'to examine the effectiveness of Land Reform Acts in protecting the beneficiaries from dispossession and exploitation. In this connection it could be said that the Land Reform Acts of all the three States under study provide sufficient protection for the beneficiaries from dispossession and exploitation provided that they are genuinely enforced and the bureaucracy is committed to safeguard the general interests of the beneficiaries. By and large, the bureaucracy seeks to protect the beneficiaries but if some cases of exploitation and dispossession come to the notice they may not be treated as a matter of serious concern as they are very small in number and in a vast society like ours such negligible cases cannot be ruled out altogether.

As regards the sixth objective, i.e. 'based on time schedule data, to assess their economic condition after becoming the beneficiaries of surplus ceiling land', it can be said that undoubtedly the beneficiaries, who are in actual possession of the land and cultivating it, have improved their socio-economic conditions substantially. The improvement in socio-economic conditions of the beneficiaries is a common phenomenon in all the three States under study. A marked change could be noticed in their food-habits, dress-habits and living conditions. They have not only improved their economic condition but a noticeable change in their social status could also be observed. Now they could freely mix up with lower middle class and could dare speak against the high-handedness of affluent and dominant sections of the society. Not only this, they also enjoy better social position among those people living below the poverty line and have not become the beneficiaries of surplus ceiling land.

As regards the seventh objective, i.e. 'whether the beneficiaries of surplus ceiling land are better off as compared to non-beneficiaries' no formal data were collected on this account as it was out of purview of the present study. However, informal discussion was held with non-beneficiaries and the beneficiaries themselves were pointedly asked as to whether they were in better financial and social position in comparison to non-beneficiaries.

Our informal discussion with non-beneficiaries and personal observation as also the reply of the beneficiaries suggest that certainly they have improved their social and economic position and they have gone ahead of non-beneficiaries.

The eighth objective was 'to locate the bottlenecks which exist in proper implementation of land reform measures and judicious distribution of surplus ceiling land'. As regards fulfilment of this objective, it is disheartening to note that due to undue political interference and administrative negligence some bottlenecks existed. For example, in Karnataka, in two to three cases it was noticed that land was assigned to three particular beneficiaries but they were not allowed to enter into their field for cultivation by some dominant people. Had the administration been alive to its responsibilities, the poor beneficiaries would not have been deprived of cultivating their land. Again, in Haryana some ex-army men had been allotted land but were not given formal possession of the land due to some procedural problems. In West Bengal, in two to three cases, it was noticed that the land which was purchased by some beneficiaries some 10 to 15 years back was declared surplus by the ex-landlords, and as a result, the poor fellows had to become the beneficiaries of surplus land though they had paid for the land. Similarly, in regard to judicious distribution of surplus ceiling land the political and administrative bottlenecks were located in a few cases in all the three States under study.

Finally, based on our empirical enquiry, the last objective was to suggest ways and means for effective and better utilization of assigned land by the beneficiaries. The fulfilment of the present objective finds a detailed discussion in the form of recommendations.

Recommendations

In view of the fulfilment of objectives of the study and the salient findings obtained, we recommend the following measures for effective distribution of surplus ceiling land and improving the socio-economic condition of assignees of surplus ceiling land. The recommendations have been divided into three heads which are as follows.

Legislative Measures

1. The following criteria may be adopted for identifying the beneficiaries for assigning surplus ceiling land:

   (i) Poorest of the poor;

   (ii) Landless agricultural labourers not engaged in any other business or profession and willing to bring the land (in the case of agricultural land) under personal cultivation;

   (iii) The beneficiary must be the resident of the village in which land has to be assigned.

   Among the eligible persons, so identified, preference may be given to the tenants/subtenants/actual cultivators of the vested land and also to the persons belonging to Scheduled Castes/Scheduled Tribes or those who form co-operative societies for the said purpose.

2. The deserving and genuine landless persons who are really interested in cultivation may be given as much quantity of land as required for minimum economic holding. At the same time, if necessary, the existing statutory ceiling limit for assigning land to the landless poor peasants may be increased.

3. For the land vested in government and to be settled in the name of the beneficiary, no premium should be charged.

4. Every State, in its Land Reform Act, should incorporate adequate punitive measures (such as eviction from the land) against the beneficiaries who fail to cultivate the land personally for consecutive three seasons and to prevent illegal transfer of land by the beneficiaries. For enforcement of such statutory measures, necessary steps should also be taken.
5. Since the big landlords often take shelter in the court of law and put resistance to the vesting of land in the State government, it may be suggested that the movement of landlords against vesting of land should be restricted to the revenue courts only and adequate steps should be taken for speedy disposal of such cases.
6. After bringing the tenants and share-croppers on the record, ownership rights may be conferred upon them. Wherever such legislative provisions are non-existant, they should be made as early as possible. After leaving sources of reasonable income for religious institutions, the State may consider conferment of ownership rights on tenants of the surplus land held by these institutions. Alternatively, a provision of an ammunity to compensate for possible loss of land be made. While conferring ownership rights on tenants, State may also consider barring lawyers from the proceedings.
7. After entering the surplus ceiling land in the record and making physical demarcation of the land, the assignees of surplus ceiling land may be given physical possession. Adequate legislative provisions should be made to provide the beneficiaries with security from eviction and to ensure prompt action for restoration of the evicted land.
8. Whenever the surplus ceiling land is assigned by the government, legal provision may be made for giving joint patta in the name of both husband and wife.

9. Necessary legislative provisions may be made in regard to patta pass with legal status and to be issued to land owners as well as tenants.
10. To identify the non-cultivable government land, the revenue department may seek the co-operation of Panchayats or the communities. The list of, so identified land, may be forwarded to DRDA/block to take up social forestry with firewocd, fruit and fodder species. Legislative provisions should also be made for granting tree pottos/leases giving usufructurary rights on trees planted and looked after by individuals on such wastelands with government, Panchayats or communities in order to involve the people in the massive greening programme of social forestry and to give them necessary incentives.

11. Administrative Measures

1. There should be a separate cell in the settlement/ block development office for maintaining the detailed records relating to the acquisition and distribution of surplus ceiling land. Such records should be maintained in pucca register separately for agricultural and non-agricultural land as also for the land used for public purposes and necessary arrangements be made for their periodical scrutiny.
2. The field study of West Bengal demonstrates the potentiality of local bodies in the implementation of land reforms. It is, therefore, suggested that the elected Panchayats should be activised to assist the administration at the grass roots level in identification, acquisition and distribution of benami and surplus ceiling land. The Panchayats may also help the government officials in protecting the beneficiaries' rights and interests against illegal dispossession or transfer of land.

3. Necessary steps should be taken for genuine selection of beneficiaries. Like Bhoomi Sahayak Samiti of the Gram Panchayats in West Bengal, there should be a separate committee of the Panchayat in every village to prepare the list of eligible beneficiaries of the locality on the criteria mentioned above. Subject to thorough verification and approval of the State government officials concerned, surplus ceiling land, as and when available, should be distributed strictly on the basis of the prepared list.
4. The government machinery at the district and block levels should keep a close and constant vigil with the help of Panchayats and local bodies so that the beneficiaries of vested land are not evicted from or dispossessed of the land. Necessary administrative and legal actions should be taken immediately after any such case of eviction or dispossession comes to the notice of the State government, officials concerned.
5. To ascertain the actual state of illegal or forceful dispossession and disposal of assigned land as also the factors responsible for them, periodical sample survey should be conducted.
6. Specially for the expeditious disposal of pending cases of litigation with revenue and other courts, an analysis of the gaps between estimated surplus, declared surplus, possession taken, land distributed as well as the disposal of pending returns should be undertaken for a time-bound remedial action.
7. To have a manageable area jurisdiction, there is a need to strengthen the revenue machinery at the village and immediate supervisory levels.
8. There is also a need for training of these persons as well as the staff engaged in survey settlement.
9. There is also a need for modernization including

computerization of land and crop based statistics on a pilot basis.

iii. Developmental Measures

Our study suggests that despite some marginal improvement in the socio-economic conditions of the deprived and downtrodden beneficiaries in terms of enhancement of their social status and the sense of dignity, distribution of surplus ceiling land has nowhere resulted in considerable and apparently visible improvement in the economic condition of the beneficiaries mainly because of the lack of follow-up actions. We, therefore, strongly recommend for taking follow-up actions to improve the economic condition of the beneficiaries. Such actions should include, inter-alia, regular and timely supply of seeds, manures, pesticides, and other agricultural inputs to the needy and deserving beneficiaries, extension of credit facilities for the purchase of costly agricultural implements and extension of irrigation facilities, particularly in drought-prone areas.

2. It is also suggested that financial subsidies of Central/State governments should be increased to make the follow-up action meaningful and result oriented.

3. A majority of the assignees of surplus ceiling lands who were interviewed, appeared to be ignorant of the credit facilities, whatsoever, available to them. It is, therefore, suggested that Panchayats and voluntary agencies should be encouraged to come up for providing necessary information to the beneficiaries about the availability of credit facilities and also helping them in completing necessary formalities to get such facilities.

4. We strongly feel that the government assistance be given in kind, and not in cash. Following the suit of Karnataka, other States may also arrange

for distribution of agricultural implements to the needy and deserving assignees through the co-operative stores. However, a small amount in cash may be given to the beneficiaries towards development of the land for agricultural purposes.

5. Where the quantity of lands available for distribution is less than the number of eligible beneficiaries, emphasis should be given on co-operative farming. However, in such cases the State government should ensure that the co-operative farms are provided with modern and sophisticated agricultural implements necessary for increasing the productivity of the land.
6. To enable the beneficiaries to improve the cultivable land, special assistance should be given to those assignees who have been assigned inferior quality of land.
7. In order to integrate the land reforms with IRDP/JRY/DPAP/DLDP, the scheme of financial; assistance to the assignees of surplus ceiling land may be implemented through the DRDAs under the full control and supervision of the PRIs.

The Ministry of Agriculture, Department of Rural Development, Government of India, as also the State governments might have taken various measures to make the land reforms a success. But, our concern ht re is confined only to giving physical possession of the surplus ceiling land to the beneficiaries, getting the mutation completed, providing agricultural inputs and ensuring the beneficiaries against forceful eviction from assigned land. We sincerely hope that if recommendations put forward here are taken into account and implemented without further delay, the economic condition of assignees of surplus ceiling land will certainly improve and they will be in a position to get two square meals for their families. In course of time, this will also improve their social status in a tradition-bound society like ours where affluence decides the social status of an individual.

Specific Recommendations

Here we would like to give some specific recommendations which may be taken care of in respect of the States covered under the study. This relates to some changes in the Land Reforms Acts of the States concerned and some general problems relating to beneficiaries of the surplus ceiling land. They are as follows:

A. West Bengal Act

1. As regards the preference to be given among the eligible persons, percentage of reservation for allotment of surplus lands to the SC/ST/Backward Classes should be specifically laid down int he Act. Section 49(1) should be amended accordingly.
2. The deserving and genuine landless peasants who are really interested in cultivation should be given as much quantity of land as required for minimum economic holding. The quantity of minimum economic holding should be specifically laid down in the Act.

B. Karnataka Act

1. Among the eligible persons for assigning surplus ceiling lands as laid down in Section 77(1), preference should be given to those who form co-operative societies for the purpose of cultivation of the assigned land.
2. For the land vested in government and to be settled in the name of the beneficiary, no premium (recoverable as arrears of land revenue or otherwise), or purchase price should be charged.

Section 78 of the Act along with related rules or provisions should be amended accordingly.

C. Haryana Act

1. Among the eligible persons for assigning surplus ceiling lands, as laid down in Section 15(2), preference should be given to those who form co-operative societies for the purpose of cultivation of the assigned lands.
2. For the land vested in government and to be settled in name of the beneficiary, no premium (recoverable as arrears of land revenue or otherwise), or purchaser price should be charged. Section 9 of the Act along with other related provision or rules should be amended accordingly.
3. Like the West Bengal and Karnataka Acts, elaborate provisions should be laid down for formation of cooperative farms and giving them certain concessions and facilities, such as reduction of land revenues, reduction of and exemption from agricultural income tax, free technical advice, financial aids and grant of subsidies and loans with or without interest and priority in irrigation from State irrigation works.

General

The criteria for assigning surplus ceiling land to the beneficiaries should be the same as given under the head 'Legislative measures'.

The suggestions put forward under the head "Development Measure" are quite elaborate and may be applicable in the case of all the three States under study.

As regards the rational scale of assistance, we recommend that Rs. 5,000 be given to the DRAP beneficiaries and Rs. 4,000 to the non-DPAP beneficiaries.

However, we strongly feel that a sum of Rs. 500 only should be given in cash towards development of land and the remaining amount should be given in kind, i.e. in the form of agricultural inputs through the block-taluk office/co-operative societies.

At the time of survey no production credit was available to beneficiaries. Banks did not co-operate and of course there were some co-operative societies in the selected districts but they did not care for the beneficiaries of surplus ceiling land.

In only rare cases, beneficiaries were assisted under the schemes of IRDP, JRY, etc. As a matter of fact, IRDP was not linked up with land reforms.

Apart from the financial assistance, the most important assistance required was the folio wing-up action of the beneficiaries and counselling from time to time. The local level bureaucratic organizations as also the enlightened citizens and NGOs can play this role most effectively.

Finally, if the recommendations given are taken into account by the government and sincerely implemented the land reforms measures may serve the purpose of social justice to a great extent.

Social Justice and Rurban Habitat

Debates on social justice evoke considerable passion—often to the extent of clouding logical judgement. The disputation concerning land reforms is no exception. In India, many powerful group of activists hold it as a self-evident truth that redistribution of land to the tiller is a must, no one should be allowed to hold much land, corporatisation of agriculture is a sin, and that the ideal is zero landless labour. All this presupposes that those who are currently engaged in agriculture should continue to do so, and that they and their progeny should do so forever and forever. Rarely is the question asked whether perpetuation of agricultural employment on the present scale is desirable—or even feasible. However blasphemous that may sound, there are a number of reasons why it is desirable to abandon the traditional fondness for giving land to the tiller.

* One, the history of modern economic development shows that in every country, without exception, agricultural employment shrinks rapidly as development proceeds. In the most advanced countries of the world, employment in agriculture is often barely two per cent of the total— and yet they have enough agricultural surplus to export, and at much lower prices than predominantly agricultural countries.
* Two, it is an inescapable rule that as an economy progresses, people spend proportionately less and less on farm products, and more and more on industrial products and on services. So, the share of the kitty that agriculture commands inexorably diminishes as the economy advances. Then, suppose, agriculture's share is reduced to 10 per cent of GNP, farmers can have the same per capita income as others and only if, farm employment shrinks to 10 per cent of the total. So, a just economic development demands that farm workers be increasingly diverted to non-farm employment, or, diverting agricultural labour is superior to any scheme of redistributing the shrinking agricultural kitty. Then, land reforms become a secondary issue; the primary concern is how to find attractive and profitable non-farm employment for redundant agricultural labour.

Three, India is currently saddled with a grain mountain of over 30 million tonnes, food is rotting in the godowns and yet little of this vast surplus can be exported because our prices are too high. The only feasible solution to this odd problem is to bring down costs, and that may be done only by increasing agricultural productivity—by reducing the number employed in agriculture.

* Four, the industrial and service sectors of the economy have started growing at substantial rates, eight per cent per year or more. In contrast, there is little or no hope that agricultural production can increase faster than two per cent or more. If this disparity continues, either farm incomes will relatively halve every decade, or farm prices should double every ten years. Neither option is sustainable.
* Five, the "moral" ground on which land reforms have been advocated—that "rich" farmers monopolise scarce land—is strictly not tenable: there is no comparable limit on non-farm income. It cannot be that only intra-rural disparity is immoral, and not rural-urban disparity! The truth is not that rich farmers are rich but that poor farm labourers are abysmally poor. That tragedy cannot be averted by doling out an acre or two of land (i.e. all that is possible with the resources available) but by getting them profitable alternative employment.
* Six, in a different vein, we do need land distribution of an entirely different type: land resettlement in such a way that each farmer gets contiguous tracts of land of viable size. Due to our inheritance laws, land has been so badly divided and subdivided that each farmer has a number of tiny disjointed bits of land. That makes it impractical for a farmer to cultivate land efficiently. In fact, one important reason why Punjab's agriculture has been as successful as it is, is because of systematic land resettlement into farms of viable size. To the extent, land resettlement improves agricultural efficiency, it will aid both farmers and farm labourers. In other words, as a parallel to minimum wage, we also need a minimum farm size—which once again means that more and more farm labour should be diverted to non-agricultural pursuits.

The Rural-Urban Divide

However, diversion of farm labour has one drawback—seasonal rural-urban migration, and the consequential trauma of social dislocation. In addition, the resultant urban explosion leads to wasteful use of scarce financial, material and human resources; causes considerable ecological damage in the bargain. Recent developments in information technology make rural-urban migration unnecessary. It would be wise to exploit such technological advancements to avoid the trauma of rural-urban migration, and the consequent drain of able and ambitious minds from villages. Instead, non-farm employment should be generated in rural areas itself. Hence, the kind of land reforms we need now are those which would transform rural economy from an agricultural to a largely non-agricultural one.

So, before we jump onto the bandwagon of land redistribution, we would be well advised to consider what our ultimate objective is: is it equal distribution of land, or is it prosperity for rural people. Equal distribution is at best one of many paths towards social justice, but it is not social justice itself. Rural social justice requires villagers to be as prosperous as townspeople; further that rural prosperity keeps pace with urban progress. Traditional land reforms are no solution for such a broad objective; instead, we need a scheme that will enable villages to generate modern industrial and service employment as well as towns and cities do.

To a certain extent, there is a realisation that redistribution of employment is necessary for economic progress, but few realise that generation of non-farm employment should be the primary goal of social justice, and that everything else—including land reforms—is secondary. In South Korea, which is the latest country to be accepted as a developed country, the share of agricultural employment dwindled from 66 per cent in 1960 to 17 per cent in 1990—a five per cent reduction per year. Currently,

India is at the same economic level South Korea was in 1966: current agricultural employment is 62 per cent—almost the same as the South Korean figure for 1960. Following the historical trend set not only by South Korea but by all developed countries, we too should systematically shrink agricultural employment. Further, if we are to develop as fast as South Korea has done, we too should aim for a five per cent annual decrease in agriculture employment, i.e. transfer about 10 million agricultural labourers each year. Such reorganisation is not a purely a rural problem; it is basically a question of rural-urban competitiveness. That is the crux of the problem: villages cannot attract businessmen and generate jobs as well as cities do.

Rurban Habitat

To appreciate the nature of the problem, consider an idealised cluster of villages spread over an area some 20 km by 20 km. Typically, that will have a population of 50 to 100 thousand people—the population of medium-sized towns. Invariably, this cluster of villages will not have the variety of services and urban amenities that a town with the same population will have, and hence, will not generate employment on the same scale. The reason for this rural-urban divide is:

NOT lack of finance because it is actually cheaper to construct schools, hospitals, commercial buildings and the like in a rural area than in an expensive town;

NOT lack of human resources because towns and cities are importers of human capital, which they can get only from villages;

NOT insufficient material resources because towns and cities usually have no raw materials at all, and rural areas have plenty.

The basic cause is, the town has a well-connected business area, a central business district, and the village cluster has none such. Because of the connectivity, towns enjoy, they can economically support a variety of social and commercial services, generate a wide range of non-farm employment. Conversely, if a cluster of villages can be designed to have a well-connected business area—an area which can be speedily, conveniently and cheaply accessed by every one in the cluster—villages too will be able to support services, industry and commerce the same way towns do. For this purpose, consider the following scheme:

* Let a dedicated bus lane be established inside the village cluster in the form of a closed loop—typically of a total length of some 50-60 km.
* Let frequent (say, every five minutes), bus services be run along this loop. As the bus lane is dedicated—it has no interfering cross traffic except at a few controlled points—the service can be fast, with average speeds of 40-50 km per hour (in our cities, bus speeds are typically no faster than 15 km per hour).

With such speeds, buses will complete the 50-60 km loop in about 80 minutes, or the maximum time distance between any two points on the bus loop will be barely 40 minutes. So, all villagers residing in the villages directly on the loop can reach any point on the bus loop within a total MAXIMUM travel time of no more than 40 minutes or so. With a smaller loop, the maximum time will be correspondingly even less.

As a result, the bus loop becomes a convenient location for a central business district. If offices, markets, industries, schools, hospitals, cinemas and the like are located on the loop, all of them will be well-connected to each other, and to substantial, urban sized populations. Hence, a large variety of service and business activity can be profitably located along the bus route. Thereby, it becomes feasible to sustain a large amount of non-agricultural employment inside what is otherwise a predominantly rural area. Such a village cluster which has a zone of high connectivity, and hence has the capability to support a large variety of urban activities, may be described as a rurban habitat. Once rurban habitats become available, there will be no need for unemployed farm labourers to migrate to cities to get jobs; they will have plenty of opportunities virtually at their own doorstep. At the most, they will have to move to a neighbouring village to get right inside a business district.

Land Reforms for Rurban Habitat

The development of rurban habitats of this type involves three preparatory steps:

* Installation of a dedicated bus lane with frequent, high speed services.
* Planned development of some 100 metres of space on either side of the bus loop in such a manner that bus movements are in no way impeded, and yet, the large number of businessmen and workers who will inevitably be attracted to such a location are well-accommodated.
* As additional seeds of development, upgradation of schools, hospitals and such other basic services all along the bus loop.

This scheme has two basic land management problems:

One, fair compensation for agricultural land diverted for rurban activities.

Two, Acquisition of Such Land Without Inordinate Delays

In India, both these problems have proved intractable with bitter accusations and counter-accusations between the bureaucracy and the people. As a result, development projects get delayed for years, and become even uneconomical only because of mounting costs of delay. That is one problem; another is, how to divert investment currently concentrated in rurban areas to these bus loops. In other words, rurban development requires a land policy which makes investment in rurban areas more attractive than in cities and towns. To resolve these difficulties, consider:

* We want zero bureaucratic interference, zero disputes: Then, let all property owners be asked to declare the surrender value of their property, the amount for which they would be willing and obliged to hand over their property to the government for any designated public cause. The owners are free to fix any value they like, however high or low; the value chosen need not have any relation to the actual cost of that property. Further, no government official can question the figure selected. So, there is no possibility of any dispute or bureaucratic interference at this stage.
* Black-marketeers are a hindrance to fast and fair development; so we want no black-market in property: Then, make the surrender value of all properties a freely available public information; allow any one to find out what it is. Next, make it obligatory for the owner to sell the property to any one who offers, say, 20 per cent more than the stated surrender value. (However, the owner can opt to retain the property by raising the surrender value to the amount that has been bid). Then, owners will be constrained by the market not to fix the surrender value at too low a level; so the black-market will collapse.
* The surrender value should not be so high as to affect public welfare projects: Then, make the taxable value of the property a function of the surrender value.
* Investors should be persuaded to move out of congested urban areas: Make the taxable value equal to the surrender value multiplied by three factors:

one, the Floor-Plot Space Ratio (commonly known as FSR or FAR); two, by the Floor-Common Property Ratio (the ratio of built up area to publicly owned space in the neighbourhood); three, an ad valorem cess if the building opens on to a thoroughfare on which public transport buses ply. Then, the tax is strictly rule based with a ten-twenty fold escalation in congested areas.

Implications

Let us consider some implications of this scheme of things. First, a palace in a village can be safely rated at a small fraction of its cost, will have its tax value further reduced because it is bound to have low FSR. In contrast, a small flat in a crowded city will be taxed at a value much higher than its cost, and that will be further aggravated because it will almost definitely be a building with high FSR. As bus routes are more common in cities, the tax load can go up even more for those who reside on busy roads. Thus tax on tax piles up as the city gets more and more congested, making it increasingly worthwhile for businessmen to shift to uncongested rurban areas where taxes will be much lower, and yet the connectivity is comparable, at any rate, sufficiently good. Then, provided the rate of congestion tax is high enough, rurban-rural reverse migration of business becomes more attractive than further escalation of urban congestion. In this manner investment in rurban areas becomes more attractive than in congested towns and cities.

Second, as explained, the primary basis of rurban attraction is the existence of a fast bus loop. Unfortunately, any such well-connected area is liable to get encroached—thereby choking off connectivity. However, the higher tax proposed on buildings opening on to bus routes will act as a deterrent against such encroachment.

Third, the option given to the owner to choose his or her own surrender value ensures that no property is expropriated by the government for a frivolous compensation, nor can an owner be harassed through long years of litigation.

Likewise, fourth, no owner can hold up a public cause by making extortionate demands and delay development through tendentious litigation. Fifth, the tax affects essentially built up land only—farm land has zero FAR and hence attracts zero tax.3 So, this wealth tax should generate no resistance in rural areas.

6

Role of Land Reform in Rural Development in the Wake of Economic Liberalisation

In the wake of the economic reform programme launched by the government of Indian in recent years, land reforms seem to have taken a back seat. This is so despite various pronouncements by the Ministry of Rural Areas and Employment that land reform continues to be one of the policy instruments for alleviation of rural poverty. Several State governments have modified their ceiling laws to exempt orchards, fish ponds, etc. there is also a move to open up tenancy for encouraging private investment in agriculture and industry. In fact, some economists argue that land market needs to be far more activised and liberalized for commercialization of agriculture and exported/demand driven agricultural growth. According to them, land reforms in the traditional sense stand against the spirit of economic reform programme which intends to promote laissez-faire/market led growth through liberalization of production and trade barriers. In reality, however, radical land reforms could be an effective aid to market led economic transformation. The present paper makes and attempt to analyse how land reform could be complementary to the economic reform programme to help build market led economic growth in Indian.

Limited Success

During the past five decades or so, the agrarian structure in India has undergone a remarkable change in the sense that all large intermediaries have been abolished and ownership right has been conferred on a considerable number of tenants. Nevertheless, the basic character of the agrarian economy with high concentration of landholdings in the hands of a few land owners on the one hand and growing number of marginal farmers and landless labourers on the other, remains more or less unaltered. The percentage share of agriculture in GDP declined from about 60 per cent in the early fifties to 30 per cent in 1992, but the proportion of agricultural labour force to total labour foce decreased only marginally from 72 per cent in the early fifties to 66 per cent in 1992. since Independence, a number of redistributive land reform measures have been undertaken to reduce the concentration ratio in the ownership and cultivation of land. But there has been limited measure of success in this regard. Not only the small and marginal farmers and landless labourers from a vast majority of the rural population, but also there is a rising trend towards marginalization of farms and casualisation of labour force. Furthermore, in the wake of the recent economic liberalisation programme, even the philosophy of re-distributive land reform is being questioned. It is often argued that the existing land reform laws restrict the growth of capitalistic/corporate farming which is necessary for market led growth. According to the protagonists of economic liberalisation, feudalistic agrarian relations have largely disappeared, without giving way to capitalistic form of farm organization, allegedly under the impact of restrictive ceiling and tenancy laws.

It has also failed to promote a socialistic or co-operative order in the agrarian economy.

Issues Involved

In view of the abovementioned facts, a number of questions arise in our mind. First of all, the most pertinent question would be: what kind of agrarian structure do we visualise for future? Do we still believe that there is need for reduction in the concentration of landholding through further redistributive land reform measures? If so, what is the scope of such redistributive land reform in future and how do we achieve this goal when we have largely failed in the past? Can we really think of the emergence of small, albeit efficient 'family farms' as the main form of farm organisation, by allowing large as well as marginal farms to disappear through appropriate policy changes. Alternatively, can we accept the reality of a growing capitalistic pattern of agrarian society in which land holdings would tend to remain concentrated in a few hands, while a majority of small and marginal farmers would be slowly converted into landless labourers? There is no denying the fact that the process of capitalistic transformation of agriculture would be painful for millions of marginal and small farmers, particularly when the existing farm and off-farm employment opportunities are inadequate to provide living income to the growing millions. Therefore, can we plan for viability and sustainability of small farms at least during the transition period? In fact, a number of institutional, technological and policy questions would have to be addressed to resolve these issues.

Distribution of Holdings: Changing Pattern

It could be seen from Table 1 that in 1950-51, about 38 per cent of operational holdings in the country were marginal holdings which operated only six per cent of the total operated area, while 5.4 per cent of the large

Table 1: Changes in the Distribution of Land Holdings in India Over Time (Per cent Share of Each Size Group)

Year	*Marginal Farm <1ha*		*Small Farm 1-2 ha*		*Semi-medium 2-4 ha*		*Medium Farm 4-10 ha*		*Large Farm >10 ha*	
	No.	*Area*	*No.*	*Area*	*No.*	*Area*	*No.*	*Area*	*No.*	*Area*
1950-51	38.4	6.0	21.7	10.2	19.2	18.2	15.3	31.6	5.4	34.0
1960-61	40.7	6.7	22.3	12.2	18.9	20.0	13.4	30.4	4.7	30.7
1970-71	50.6	9.0	19.1	11.9	15.2	18.5	11.2	29.7	3.9	30.91
1976-77	54.6	10.7	18.0	12.8	14.3	19.9	10.1	30.4	3.0	26.2
1980-81	56.4	12.1	18.1	14.1	14.0	21.2	19.1	29.6	2.4	23.0
1985-86	57.8	13.4	18.4	15.6	13.6	22.3	8.2	28.6	2.0	20.1
1990-91	59.0	14.9	19.0	17.3	13.2	23.2	7.2	27.2	1.6	17.4

farms above 10 ha, cultivated 34 per cent of the total area. According to the 1990-91 agricultural census, the proportions of marginal farms increased to 59 per cent which shared about 15 per cent of the total area. But large farms formed only 1.6 per cent of the total holdings and 17.4 percent of the total area. Still only about 8.6 per cent of large and medium farms at the top bracket cultivate nearly 45 per cent of the total land. Thus, even if we compare the pre-land reform year of 1950-51 with 1990-91, the series of land reform measures during the past four decades do not seem to have improved the pattern of land distribution. In 1990-91, about 1.6 per cent of farms at the top bracket cultivated 17.4 percent of the total land, whereas in 1950-51, nearly 5.4 per cent of farms at the top bracket operated 34 per cent of the total land. In fact, the pattern of land distribution seems to have been more skewed in recent years. It could be further seen from Table 2 that the average size of land of various size groups of farms did not significantly change over time. During the last two agricultural census periods, however, the average sizes of large as well as marginal and small farms slightly increased, while that of medium-sized group of farms declined. Table-3 shows the average size of marginal, small and large farms in various States over time. Tables 4 and 5 indicate the continued skewness in the pattern of distribution of operational holdings in various States during 1970-71 to 1990-91. The results of various rounds of National Sample Survey (Table 6) also show similar rising trends in the concentration ratio of ownership and operational holdings over time.

Growth of Landlessness

According to the recent rounds of National Sample Survey, the proportions of landless households increased from 9.6 per cent in 1971-72 to 14.4 percent in 1987-88. Table 7, however, shows that during 1981 to 1987, the proportions of landless households to total rural households declined in several States including Assam, Jammu & Kashmir, Karnataka, Kerala, Madhya Pradesh, Manipur, Orissa, Tripura and West Bengal. In all other States, there was a slightly rising trend in the proportion of landless households. Also, in several States including Andhra Pradesh, Bihar, Gujarat, Madhya Pradesh, Maharashtra, Punjab and Tamil Nadu, more than 10 per cent of rural households did not possess owned homestead land. Recent rounds of National Sample Survey data further revealed that the proportion of casual labour to the total rural work-force increased from 22 per cent in 1972-73 to 31.4 per cent in 1987-88 in the case of male work-force and from 31.4 per cent to 35.5 per cent in the case of female workers. Thus, given the past trends to continue, the increasing number of marginal farmers and landless labourers including casual labourers would swell the rank of rural poor. Small and semi-medium farms also numbered about 32 per cent and cultivated above 41 per cent of the total land. In fact, it is the strong attachment of small and"semi-medium farmers with land who also happen to maintain their farm efficiency at relatively higher levels which prevent the rapid growth of capitalist farming and not so much the restrictive land reform laws which in any way remained mostly ineffective.

Land Reforms and Economic Liberalisation

As India's IInd Five Year Plan put it, the major objectives

Table 2: Changes in the Average Size of Operational Holdings Over Tune in India

Size Group	*Average Size*					
	1960-61	*1970-71*	*1976-77*	*1980-81*	*1985-86*	*1990-91*
Marginal (<1 ha)	0.44	0.41	0.39	0.39	0.38	0.40
Small (1-2 ha)	1.47	1.44	1.42	1.44	1.43	1.44
Semi-Medium (2-4 ha)	2.84	2.81	2.78	2.78	2.76	2.76
Medium (4-10 ha)	6.10	6.08	6.04	6.04	5.94	5.90
Large (Above 10 ha)	17.48	18.07	17.57	17.41	17.20	17.33
Overall	2.69	2.30	2.00	1.84	1.69	1.57

Table 3: Changes in the Average Size of Marginal Small and Large Holdings by State
Average Size (ha)

Marginal	Small (less than 1 ha)		(1-2 ha)		Large (above 10 ha)		Average of nil groups	
	1970-71	1990-91	1970-71	1990-91	1970-71	1990-91	1970-71	1990-91
1. Andhra Pradesh	0.44	0.45	0.44	0.43	17.87	25.61	2.31	1.51
2. Assam	0.45	0.41	0.42	0.39	57.31	78.08	1.47	1.31
3. Bihar	0.40	0.37	0.40	0.41	17.50	15.99	1.50	0.93
4. Gujarat	0.52	0.53	0.47	0.47	15.56	16.41	4.11	2.93
5. Haryana	0.49	0.47	0.44	0.52	15.86	15.43	3.77	2.43
6. Himachal Pradesh	0.38	0.41	0.48	0.36	23.78	18.11	1.53	1.20
7. Jammu & Kashmir	0.41	0.38	0.46	0.38	18.75	23.00	0.94	0.83
8. Karnataka	0.51	0.47	0.45	0.46	16.44	15.22	3.20	2.13
9. Kerala	0.23	0.18	0.31	0.36	46.67	55.74	0.57	0.33
10. Madhya Pradesh	0.40	0.45	0.45	0.50	17.60	16.46	4.00	2.63
11. Maharashtra	0.47	0.49	0.46	0.46	16.47	15.17	4.28	2.21
12. Manipur	0.53	0.55	0.18	0.37	14.04	12.16	1.15	1.23
13. Meghalaya	0.70	0.54	0.50	0.32	10.70	14.25	1.70	1.76
14. Nagaland	0.65	0.64	0.23	0.40	18.4	16.63	5.40	6.84
15. Orissa	0.52	0.49	0.53	0.38	16.43	16.61	1.89	1.34
16. Punjab	0.44	0.56	0.43	0.61	15.49	16.03	2.89	3.61
17. Rajasthan	0.49	0.48	0.45	0.44	22.30	19.13	5.46	4.11
18. Tamil Nadu	0.42	0.36	0.42	0.41	16.94	18.44	1.45	0.93
19. Tripura	0.40	0.40	0.41	0.53	33.53	121.57	1.02	0.97
20. UP	0.37	0.38	1.40	0.41	16.08	15.34	1.16	090
21. West Bengal	0.43	0.45	1.53	1.44	64.20	156.99	1.20	0.90
22. All-India	0.40	1.38	0.40	1.44	18.15	17.33	2.28	1.57

of agrarian reforms are:

(i) To provide the social, economic and institutional framework for agricultural growth with social justice,

(ii) Remove such impediments to agricultural production as arise from the character of the agrarian structure, and

(iii) To create conditions for, as speedily as possible, an agrarian economy with high levels of efficiency and produc-avity. Now on similar grounds of efficiency and productivity being emphasised. The proclaimed objectives of both land reform and ongoing economic reform programmes are to liberate the productive forces in agriculture and develop an efficient agricultural production system. However, the routes and implications of land reform and economic reform programmes are different. First, while land reform intends to promote both agricultural growth and equity, the economic reform programme does not talk about equity. Secondly, land reform intends to release initiatives for development of both agriculture and industry through development of internal market, local entrepreneurship and democratisation of the rural society, whereas the present economic reform programme relies more on global entrepreneurship including multinationals and export led agricultural growth. The most pertinent question is under what conditions of social organisation and in which institutional system does the market work more efficiently. Given the unequal agrarian structure and imperfect market in rural India, economic reforms may benefit traders, multinational corporations and large farmers and would in all probability harm the interest of small and marginal farmers and landless people would become more helpless and dependent en big farmers and

Table 4: Changes in the Number of Operational Holdings Over Time (by State)

Sl.No.	State	% Share in the number of total operational holdings									
		Marginal		*Small*		*Semi-medium*		*Medium*		*Large*	
		1970	*1990*	*1970*	*1990*	*1970*	*1990*	*1970*	*1990*	*1970*	*1990*
1.	Andhra Pradesh	46.0	56.1	19.6	21.2	174	14.5	12.7	6.9	4.3	1.3
2.	Assam	57.0	60.0	23.8	22.6	14.0	13.4	4.8	3.8	0.4	0.2
3.	Bihar	64.3	76.6	14.6	11.3	12.1	8.1	7.2	3.4	1.8	0.4
4.	Gujarat	23.8	26.3	19.1	26.0	22.8	35.3	24.7	19.0	9.6	3.4
5.	Haryana	27.4	40.7	18.9	19.9	22.5	20.0	23.1	14.5	8.1	3.0
6.	Himachal Pradesh	58.2	63.7	20.2	19.9	14.2	11.4	6.3	4.4	1.1	0.7
7.	Jammu & Kashmir	72.8	74.1	15.8	16.2	8.8	8.0	2.5	1.6	0.1	0.1
8.	Karnataka	39.2	23.6	27.5	22.2	20.1	17.5	11.0	6.2	2.2	
9.	Kerala	84.9	92.6	9.5	5.2	4.5	1.8	0.9	0.4	0.2	0.1
10.	Madhya Pradesh	31.8	37.3	16.8	22.8	20.1	20.7	20.0	15.3	9.3	3.8
11.	Maharashtra	25.1	34.6	17.7	28.8	22.0	22.4	24.8	12.4	12.4	1.8
12.	Meghaiaya	36.8	34.5	34.6	29.8	24.1	26.9	4.3	7.6		
13.	Orissa	43.3	53.6	32.9	26.2	13.3	15.0	9.1	4.7	1.4	0.4
14.	Punjab	37.6	26.5	18.9	18.3	20.4	25.9	18.0	23.4	5.0	6.0
15.	Rajasthan	29.7	18.5	20.0	20.7	20.8	21.5	19.9	14.0	9.7	
16.	Tamil Nadu	58.8	73.1	20.9	15.9	13.1	7.7	6.1	2.9	1.1	0.4
17.	UP	66.8	73.8	17.2	15.5	10.6	7.7	4.7	2.7	2.7	0.2
18.	West Bengal	60.0	73.8	22.3	17.6	13.2	7.3	4.4	1.3	0.1	0.02
19.	All-India	50.9	59.0	18.9	19.0	15.0	13.2	11.4	7.2	3.8	1.6

contractors, thereby leaving no scope for equal participation of the poor in the democratic functioning of the country. Besides, because of capital-intensive nature of industrial growth and lack of necessary skill on lively by coercing the landless and marginal farmers who do not have necessary skills and resources to take up new things more effectively (who in all probability contribute to urban slums only) or pressurise the rural rich to migrate who have relatively greater access to human as well as financial resources which are so necessary for any efficient entry into new areas. The landlords have often high levels of income which place them on the backward bending position of their supply of effort function. With radical land distribution, there will occur wealth redistribution which would impel the former land owning class to rely for income creation on their entrepreneurial abilities rather than their wealth.

The experience of countries like Japan and Korea shows that land reform can help in the faster and more sustainable development of capitalism, without creating so much pain for the working class. But market led economic reform without being accompanied by land reform would be painful for the rural working class and may not sustain in the long run. In the part of the poor village workers, there may not be enough scope for migration and absorption of the growing rural workforce in the industrial sector. Hence the best proposition would be to implement land reforms for allowing the agricultural labourers to cultivate land and pressurise the land owning class to leave agriculture and undertake non-agricultural occupation. Even if we assume that there is a limit beyond which agriculture cannot absorb and contain such a huge proportion of small and marginal farmers as well as landless labourers and that there is need for rapid transfer of population from agriculture to non-agriculture, our policy goal should be made far more clear whether we can

Table 4: Changes in the Number of Operational Holdings Over Time (by State)

Sl.No.	State	% Share in the number of total operational holdings									
		Marginal		Small		Semi-medium		Medium		Large	
		1970	1990	1970	1990	1970	1990	1970	1990	1970	1990
1.	Andhra Pradesh	8.0	16.4	11.3	19.6	19.2	25.2	30.8	26.1	30.7	12.8
2.	Assam	17.7	19	22.9	24.1	26.3	27.6	18	15.2	15.1	14.1
3.	Bihar	16	30.3	13.6	17.1	22.1	23.8	27.6	21	20.7	7.7
4.	Gujarat	3	4.8	6.8	13	16	24.4	37.8	38.9	36.5	18.9
5.	Haryana	3.5	7.9	7.2	12.5	17	25.4	37.1	35	34.2	19.1
6.	Himachal Pradesh	14.5	21.5	19	22.5	25.7	25.7	23.7	20.4	17.1	9.9
7.	Jammu & Kashmir	32.1	34.2	24.6	26.8	26.1	260	14.7	10.7	2.5	2.3
8.	Karnataka	4.8	8.7	10.7	18.7	19.4	26	33.4	30.6	31.7	16
9.	Kerala	34.4	48.8	22.7	21.1	21.1	14.1	9.3	6.3	12.5	9.7
10.	Madhya Pradesh	3.4	6.4	6.2	12.6	14.5	21.9	34.7	39.1	41.2	24
11.	Maharashtra	2.7	7.7	6.1	19	14.8	28.1	36.4	32.8	40	12.4
12.	Meghalaya		14.9	10.6	31.1	22.5	38.9	38.7	13.8	23.8	
13.	Orissa	12	19.7	26.6	26.9	21.1	29.5	27.8	19.1	12.5	4.8
14.	Punjab	5.7	4.1	9.4	8.1	20	20	38.1	40.2	26.9	26.7
15.	Rajasthan	2.2	3.5	4.9	7	11	14.4	24.7	30.2	52.2	44.9
16.	Tamil Nadu	17.1	28.3	?ns	tA.fl	1AS.	T3.&	lA.t,	V//b	tj.-u	-in
17.	UP	21.1	31.4	20.8	24.4	25.0	24.4	23.2	16.9	9.0	3.9
18.	West Bengal	21.5	36.5	25.7	30.0	28.9	28.4	29.2	7.5	4.7	5.6
19.	All-India	9.0	14.9	11.9	17.3	18.5	23.2	29.7	27.2	30.9	17.4

influence migration more effecother words, market led economic reform does not provide an alternative to radical land reform. In fact, land reform should precede market reform as a means for rapid and balanced economic development. It needs to be clearly borne in mind that rural underdevelopment in India is not merely a function of resource allocation as determined by the market mecha nism. It is more a product of unequal agrarian structure, including the power structure. It has been observed that in about 70 per cent cases, the countries which introduced Structural Adjustment Programme (SAP) since 1980, have witnessed a decline in food production per capita (Ghonemy, 1990). Studies by Cornia et al (1987) and Singh (1986) show that countries like China, Botswana, Egypt, South Korea and Zimbabwe which have relatively egalitarian agrarian structure due to implementation of land reforms, maintained a good record of food production, economic growth and high levels of public expenditure on health and education. But countries like Argentina, Brazil, Chile, Costa Rica and Kenya (where the concentration ratio of ownership and cultivation of land were very high), poverty and income distribution worsened. The poor suffered due to three to four digits inflation and drastic reduction in food subsidies as well as public expenditure on health and education. The decline in food production also constrained the overall pace of rural development. Another recent study (Amponsah and Hushak, 1992), shows that in sub-Saharan Africa, formal macroeconomic structural adjustment may not be a necessary requirement in effecting efficient performance in the agriculture sector. Moreover, offering national treatment to foreign investors may create conditions for greater drain of foreign exchange resources, thereby defeating the main objective of SAP. (EPQ, Jan. 25, 1992). Many of the Latin American Countries continue to be in the heavy debt trap, despite their several years of structural reform experience.

Scope for Further Reform

The available data suggest that there are hardly one lakh acres of ceiling surplus land available for redistribution. Even if we include the surplus land under litigation or reserved for public purposes, this will make hardly 2.57

Table 6: Changes in the Concentration Ratio (Gini Coefficient) of Ownership and Operational Holdings from 1971 to 1991

JteK	*Gini coefficient Ownership*			*Operational Holdings*		
	1971	*1981*	*1991*	*1971*	*1981*	*1991*
Andhra Pradesh	0.732	0.736	0.740	0.606	0.599	0.592
Assam	0.622	0.556	0.490	0.422	0.519	0.616
Bihar	0.719	0.686	0.653	0.556	0.606	0.656
Gujarat	0.683	0.696	0.703	0.540	0.558	0.576
Haryana	0.753	0.699	0.645	0.464	0.598	0.732
Himachal Pradesh	0.546	0.541	0.536	0.586	0.468	0.356
Jammu & Kashmir	0.425	0.519	0.613	0.397	0.460	0.523
Karnataka	0.663	0.685	0.707	0.527	0.581	0.635
Kerala	0.702	0.681	0.660	0.647	0.649	0.651
Madhya Pradesh	0.621	0.647	0.673	0.533	0.535	0.537
Maharashtra	0.687	0.697	0.712	0.526	0.571	0.616
Meghalaya	0.476	0.480	0.484	0.383	0.436	0.489
Orissa	0.645	0.614	0.583	0.501	0.526	0.551
Punjab	0.776	0.767	0.758	0.418	0.702	0.986
Rajasthan	0.607	0.616	0.625	0.564	0.604	0.644
Tamil Nadu	0.751	0.756	0.760	0.516	0.640	0.764
Tripura	0.539	0.609	0.879	0.472	0.547	0.622
UP	0.631	0.604	0.577	0.495	0.565	0.635
West Bengal	0.672	0.633	0.594	0.490	0.597	0.704
All-India	0.710	0.713	0.716	0.586	0.629	0.672

Table 7: Changes in the Proportions of Landless Labourers

Sl. No.	State	Proportion of landless rural house			
		1971-72	1981	1987-88	without owned homestead
1.	Andhra Pradesh	46.6	11.9	15.30	10.9
2.	Assam	25.0	7.5	2.5	2.3
3.	Bihar	4.3	4.1	12.0	10.6
4.	Gujarat	13.4	16.8	27.3	17.8
5.	Haryana	11.9	6.1	7.5	6.1
6.	Himachal Pradesh	4.4	7.7	8.8	7.8
7.	Jammu & Kashmir	1.0	6.8	3.4	3.3
8.	Karnataka	12.5	13.7	12.6	7.7
9.	Kerala	15.7	12.8	5.3	5.0
10.	Madhya Pradesh	9.6	14.4	13.1	12.2
11.	Maharashtra	10.4	21.2	27.0	20.9
12.	Manipur	5.8	2.1	0.6	0.5
13.	Orissa	10.6	7.7	5.1	4.6
14.	Punjab	7.1	6.4	27.5	24.6
15.	Rajasthan	2.9	8.1	9.7	7.5
16.	Tamil Nadu	17.0	19.1	20.3	18.4
17.	Tripura	11.4	14.9	9.1	8.9
18.	UP	4.6	4.9	11.5	7.8
19.	West Bengal	9.8	16.2	13.4	9.6
	All-India	9.6	11.3	14.4	11.1

lakh acres of land available for redistribution. But if the ceiling law is partly revised and lowered, the acreage under ceiling surplus land could be enhanced. According to a rough estimate, if the ceiling is fixed at four ha uniformly, there will be about 36.7 million ha of land above ceiling, according to 1990-91 agricultural census. At the top bracket, there are about 9.3 million holdings, operating nearly 73.9 million ha of land. If we leave four ha with each of such holdings, the surplus land would be of that high order. But at present, there is no 'political

Table 8: Progress in the Implementation of Ceiling Laws (Up to December 1994)

State	*Area declared*	*Area reserved for public purposes*	*No. of beneficiaries*	*Area distributed*	*Area transferred*	*Total cases in courts*	*Area unfit for cultivation*	*Net area available for distribution*
Andhra Pradesh	806.9	555.4		483.9	21.9	175.2	10.6	7.6
Assam	612.4	491.5		434.1	17.2	38.5	13.1	38.0
Bihar	489.4	295.0		359.0	1.7	161.0	18.6	4.5
Gujarat	246.2	132.2		284.0	3.3	30.6	25.6	4.4
Haryana	92.3	82.1		80.7	5.7	2.6	1.1	
Himachal Pradesh	9.2	0.2		214.1	22.8	4.5	4.2	
Jammu & Kashmir	455.6	450.0		—	0	0	5.6	
Kamataka	273.1	116.5		30.8	14.0	142.5	0	0.3
Kerala	136.9	64.2		144.5	20.4	28.0	0	0
Madhya Pradesh	291.5	85.1		72.1	5.5	37.4	19.9	2.0
Maharashtra	727.6	551.4		140.1	100.6	0.05	0	0.2
Manipur	1.8	1.7		1.3	0	H.I	2.2	0
Orissa	174.5	152.7		132.6	3.0	30.0	0	0.7
Punjab	132.6	102.5		26.7	68.0	66.6	10.0	0.1

Rajasthan	599.6	441.8	77.1	9.7	34.2	0	8.2
Tamil Nadu	188.4	154.2	128.9	73.0	20.2	0.9	0.1
Tripura	2.0	1.6	1.4	0.2	0.4	0.06	0
UP	544.9	371.4	32.4	34.6	173.5	0.9	0.9
West Bengal	1,271.0	947.7	2.0	3.4	13	323.2	0.8
D&NHaveli	9.4	6.9	85.0	78.3	25	69.0	0.1
Delhi	1.1	0.4	0.9	—	0.7	0	0.16
Pondicherry	2.4	1.0	1.4	—	13	0	0.03
All-India	7343.3	5108.8	5,957.1	385.8	1,186.7	380.5	100.7

Area - '000 acres; 2. No. = '000 persons.

will' on the part of various State governments to go in for such revision of ceiling laws. In fact, uniform ceiling of four ha would prevent manipulation through change of land classification and would also make it possible for the small, albeit family farm norms to emerge. Table 9 shows the estimated ceiling surplus land by State, on the basis of the above criterion. Besides, there are about 15 million ha of government wasteland which can be liberated from illegal encroachment and redistributed among the landless and semi-landless poor. This would enhance their economic capabilities and overall sustainability.

Viability and Sustainability of Small Farms

In view of the predominance of efficient small family farms in the agrarian structure, it is necessary to ensure the viability and sustainability of small farms. Our recent survey results from eight selected districts of Anantpur and West Godavari (AP), Bhagalpur and Patna (Bihar) Bhiwani and Karnal (Haryana), and Sri Ganganagar and Bikaner (Rajasthan) show that small and medium farms still produce comparatively more per unit of land than large as well as marginal farms in most places. Nevertheless, marginal and small farmers invariably stay below the poverty line in all the selected districts, except ing in the relatively developed district of Karnal in Haryana and West Godavari in Andhra Pradesh (Haque, NIRD, 1993). In other words, small farms turn out to be viable and sustainable only in those areas where irrigation facilities are available and help in improving the cropping intensity and technology absorption capacity of small farms. Besides, small farms which diversified their activities including the cultivation of cereals, fruit, vegetables, plantations, sericulture and livestock farming earned comparatively more and stable income than those who depended mainly on cereal crops.

Integrating Small Farms with Non-farm Development

Agriculture cannot sustain the growing millions of marginal and small farmers. Therefore, it would be necessary to integrate small farms with non-farm development. However, the latest available data show that the proportion of non-farm workers in rural areas increased only marginally from 18.9 per cent in 1981 to 19.8 per cent in 1991.

Conclusion

In view of the slow growth of capitalistic farming, small and marginal family farms would continue to be the most dominant form of farm organisation in India in the years to come. Therefore, appropriate technological, institutional, organisational and policy changes for ensuring viability and sustainability of small farms would be necessary. The following points may serve as guidelines in this direction:

1. The results of ICAR's National Demonstrations show that there is huge untapped technological/ yield potentials in respect of various crops in almost all parts of the country. Bridging of such technological gap by increasing the small farmers' access to improved technology would enhance the viability of small farms. Therefore, identification and bridging of technological gaps in both irrigated and unirrigated areas by involving small farms and development of appropriate technologies for dry/ rainfed areas should be given topmost priority in the strategy of future agricultural development.
2. Given the present pressure of population on land to continue, the average size of small and marginal farms may decline. Radical redistribution of land could have helped in improving the marginal farmer's access to land. But the past experience in this regard has not been very satisfactory. According to the latest available data (as of December, 1994),

there are hardly one lakh acres of ceiling surplus land available for redistribution, excluding the 1.57 million acres of lands which are under litigation or reserved for public purposes. However, wastelands constitute nearly 20 per cent of the total geographical area in India which could be reclaimed and distributed among the landless and semi-landless people, for crop farming, agro-forestry and social forestry. There are about 15 million ha of culturable wastelands and 26 million ha of fallow lands which can be acquired, reclaimed and distributed for providing adequate income and employment opportunities to the marginal farmers and landless labourers. It has been estimated that on an average, it requires about Rs. 5 ,486 to reclaim one ha of culturable wasteland and put it into cultivation. Thus, with about Rs. 22,000 crore of investment, we can convert all our 62 million marginal farms into small farms above one ha and alternatively, if these wastelands are distributed among small farms, it would increase their viability. In the absence of adequate ceiling surplus land, regeneration and redistribution of wasteland and fallow lands would be the only way to increase small and marginal farmer's access to land for their viability plantation crops. However, strong government as well as co-operative support for technology, training, capital, market, transportation and other infrastructures would be essential for such diversification of small farms.

3. Agricultural sector in India can hardly afford to sustain all its growing population and therefore, vertical diversification of small farms is all the more important, involving adequate development of non-farm activities. But the investment and organisational requirements of such vertical diversification in the form of participation of small farms in agro-industry, agri-business, agro-

processing and services would be even greater. Also, this may require the emergence of contract farming without compromising with small farmers' security of land ownership and co-operative/ collaborative efforts of government/private corporate sector, farmers' cooperatives and NGOs for such vertical diversification to bear fruits.

Table 9

Estimates of Ceiling Surplus land by State (Area '000 ha)

State	*Area declared surplus*	*Area estimated to be (upto Dec., 1994) ceiling surplus**
Andhra Pradesh	327	2,577
Assam	248	534
Bihar	198	1,308
Gujarat	997	2,798
Haryana	37	937
Himachal Pradesh	115	135
Jammu & Kashmir	184	47
Karnataka	111	2,682
Kerala	55	191
Madhya Pradesh	118	6,641
Maharashtra	295	4,076
Orissa	71	460
Punjab	54	1,387
Rajasthan	243	9,716
Tamil Nadu	76	839
Uttar Pradesh	221	1,364
West Bengal	515	309
All-India	2,973	36,746

* Based on 4 ha as the uniform ceiling on all types of land.

Table 10

Proportion of Wasteland to Total Geographical Area by State

State	*% of Wasteland*
Andhra Pradesh	19.6
Assam	57.0
Bihar	17.4
Gujarat	17.6
Haryana	5.4
Himachal Pradesh	37.7
Jammu & Kashmir	47.7
Karnataka	15.2
Kerala	5.3
Madhya Pradesh	20.9
Maharashtra	20.8
Manipur	54.2
Nagaland	53.5
Orissa	16.0
Punjab	2.5
Rajasthan	34.0
Tamil Nadu	16.0
Uttar Pradesh	10.2
West Bengal	7.8
All-India	20.1

Land Reforms : Key to Rural Uplift in North-East India

The basic fact that rural uplift in North-East India in particular and our country in general cannot be divorced from land reforms, is realized by all of us today. It may be noted that one of the demands made by different ethnic groups in Assam while launching the campaign for autonomy, is the protection of their land. This region is very fertile for horticulture, sericulture and small-scale industries. All these are directly connected with land. Further, Assam occupies a unique position in the world for production of tea and more than 80 per cent rural people depend on agriculture and allied activities for their livelihood. This paper is an attempt to analyse the problem of rural uplift and land reforms in North-East India.

North-East India, situated in a corner of India, has natural frontiers on three sides. Her northern frontier from the Sankosh river on the west to the entrance of the mighty Brahmaputra is guarded by the Assam Himalayas. The Macmahon Line separates North-East India from Tibet. In the west, the region is bounded by Bhutan, Tibet and China in the north-east, Burma in the south-east and Bangladesh in the south:

Geographical Area

State	*Area (sq km)*
Arunachal Pradesh	83,740
Assam	78,523
Manipur	22.356
Meghalaya	22,429
Mizoram	21,087
Nagaland	16,531
Tripura	10,478
North-East India	2,55,144

North-East India accounts for 7.7 per cent of the country's total land area and has a population-representing 3.88 per cent of the country's total population. The hill area covers 70 per cent of the total land area of the region.

It may be noted that though the region is well-known for its physical, social, economic and political diversities, but there is a common factor which permeates the whole region. That common factor is the underdevelopment of the rural area. The bulk of the rural sector has remained untouched by the developmental programmes earned out for more than four decades. A little more than 80 per cent workers are engaged in agriculture and allied activities for their livelihood. Therefore, the uplift of rural areas in the

North-East region is dependent on land reform or land protection or land distribution among the rural people:

DISTRIBUTION OF POPULATION: RURAL AND URBAN

State	*Total*	*Rural*	*Urban*	*% of Urban population*
Arunachal Pradesh	6,31,839	5,90,411	41,428	6.56
Assam	1,98,96,843	1,78,49,657	10,47,186	10.29
Manipur	14,20,953	13,35,819	10,45.493	26.42
Meghalaya	10,94,486	3,75,460	2,41.333	18.07
Mizoram	4.93.757	3,71,943	1.21.814	24.67
Nagaland	7,74,930	6,54,969	1,20.234	15.52
Tripura	20,52,058	8,27,460	2,25,568	10.99

Community Ownership of Land

In most hill areas of North-East India, the land is owned by the community as a whole. However, individual ownership of land is recognized in certain areas, but such ownership is usually confined to homestead and settled farm land. Generally, each village is considered as one unit and within the village the village headman or the Council is the authority to distribute land for cultivation among the individual families.

Role of headman : A brief survey shows that among the Karbis and some tribes of Arunachal Pradesh, though there is the provision for community ownership, one can cultivate a plot of land according to his choice. The village headman generally settles disputes relating to sharing of jhum land among the villagers. Sometimes if a particular group is not satisfied with the decision of the headman it leaves the original village and establishes a new village with a new headman. In the Garo Hills of Meghalaya, the hill mouzas are divided into several aking and each aking is placed under the control of a Nokma (headman). He owns land on behalf of his clansmen. He can distribute the land among the clansmen for jhuming. The district of Khasi Hills of Meghalaya is divided into Rajs ruled by Siems, Lyndoh, Pator and Sardar. Each member of the Raj is entitled to cultivate any vacant land. As long as he cultivates, the vacant land belongs to him. If a man does not cultivate the land under his control for three years continuously, he loses right to cultivate in it and the land becomes the property of Raj.

Jhuming: In the hill areas, the shifting cultivation or jhuming is a system of production and a way of life of the people. This system was followed for a long time as a regular system by the inhabitants of Africa, America, Sweden, Brazil, etc. In India, shifting cultivation is practised throughout the hill areas covering the States in North-East India, Sikkim, Orissa, Bihar, Madhya Pradesh, Andhra Pradesh, Tamil Nadu, Maharashtra and Kerala.

The shifting cultivation involves cutting and burning of weed, even forests, growing of a mixture of different crops, viz. paddy, maize, cotton, millet and vegetables of various kinds on the cleared land with lowest possible technology under rainfed condition and shifting to a new site next year. The burning causes substantial reduction in organic matter content of the soil. Again leaving land in fallow for a couple of years means a great national waste. It also widens the gap between the food grains production under jhum cultivation and the number of jhumias dependent on it.

The North-Eastern Council in its Fifth Plan took up eight pilot projects for the settlement of jhumias at a cost of Rs. 497 lakh till March 1979. The governments of Assam, Arunachal Pradesh, Nagaland, Meghalaya, Mizoram and Tripura have also tried in several ways to eliminate jhuming. Despite all the efforts of the State governments and the North-Eastern Council, jhum cultivation remains as a serious problem and calls for a well integrated and co-ordinated approach involving disciplines of horticulture, agriculture, animal husbandry, forestry, soil and water conservation, engineering, technology, rural sociology, etc.

Thus the whole gamut of the rural society in hill areas is interwoven by this shifting cultivation system. It is deep-rooted agriculture. The hill tribes of North-East India produce various agricultural products in their jhum field. They produce food grains, vegetables and also cash crops. On the other hand, it damages the forest. It dries up the springs of the hills, causes soil waste and erosion and destroys valuable forests.

Tribal ethos & land reforms: The difficulty lies in the formulation of a new policy relating to land in two factors:

1) The evaluation of economic benefit out of production im jhum field and the damage caused by it to forests and soil.
2) Socio-cultural aspect of the hill tribes. Any new polio on Sand for their uplift cannot ignore the cultural sensitiveness of the tribal society.

The Assam Scenario

In Assam, the rural people in the plain areas depend or agriculture and allied activities which constitute their mar provision and it involves land as a primary factor for their: uplift. During the Ahom rule in the State, the system of State ownership of lands was prevalent. The Ahom king used to grant lands to idols, Brahmins, religious institutions and elite groups devoted to learning and administration. AD the grants were grouped into three categories : 1) *Debottor.* dedication to idols or temples. This grant was further subdivided into two groups—*Bhogdani* and *Paikan.* The owners of *Bhogdani* land had to supply daily ration to the temple and the owners of the *Paikan* land had to render personal service to the kingdom;

2) *Dharmottor,* dedication to person for service, to be rendered to the temples; and 3) *Brahmottor,* dedication to priests.

Besides, there was the *Paik* system organised by Momai Tamuly Barbaruah. Under this system, every male adult with good physical health had to render free service to the State, either as a labourer or soldier or as supplier of certain quantity of produce in lieu there of. He was called *Paik.* The *Paiks* were organised into *Gets.* Each *Get* contained three or four *Paiks.* Each *Paik* rendered service to the king on rotation. In return, each *Paik* was allotted eight bighas of rice land. He was also given land for his house and gardens, called *bari* and *bari* land.

The British, at the time of annexation of Assam, welcomed the State ownership system. The British brought into existence the historic permanent settlement confirming decennial settlement of Bengal. The zamindari privileges continued to exist till the enactment of the State Acquisition of Zamindari Act, 1951.

Assam Tenancy Reforms Legislation

In Independent India, land reforms received top priorit) in order to put an end to the zamindari system and the landed intermediaries together with conferment of tenancy rights to ryots bringing them in direct relationship with the State instead. While the rest of Assam where temporal? settled estates existed, the Assam (Temporarily settled Areas) Tenancy Act, 1971 and it was extended to Goalpara also. The Asssam Land Holding Act, 1974 was enacted with the aim of bringing tenants under the direct relationship with the State.

The Assam Land Holding Act, 1974 is a landmark in the history of land reform in particular and rural uplift in general. It provides for a single system of landholders under which owners of land have been put under contract with the State as settlement holder directly enjoying rights and privileges and with the obligation of payment of land revenue direct to the State instead of any zamindar. Thus it may be seen that efforts have been made by the government to simplify the land tenure system in Assam.

Land ceiling and distribution: Coming to the ceiling law, an area of 50 bighas has been considered as a standard area for the livelihood of an average family. As a result, whoever has more lands than 50 bighas has a surplus. The government acquires this surplus and then distributes it among persons with no lands or with lands less than the ceiling.

Till now, 6,12,380 acres of land have been declared surplus and of these, 5,75,837 acres have been acquired by the government. So far, 4,91,301.70 acres have been distributed. The following table shows the details:

SURPLUS LAND DISTRIBUTION

(in acres)

	No. of families	*Area distributed*
S.Cs.:	42,490	44,360.03
S.Ts.:	41,291	57,794.54
Others:	3,49,519	3,67,960.59
Institutions:	610	21,186.54
Total		4,91,301.70

Area unfit for distribution	13,106.00
Area under litigation	38,461.00
Area under encroachment	10,275.00
Area reserved for public use	17,250.00
Area under miscellaneous reasons	4,006.00
Area available for distribution	37,980.30

Source : Status paper for the workshop on land reforms held on 3-5 April, 1995 submitted by Mr N.K. Chetia, Director of Land Requisition and Reform; Govt. of Assam.

Floods: A Major Problem

Rural uplift is severely affected in the plain areas of Assam due to floods of which the mighty Brahmaputra and Barak are the main sources. The Brahmaputra flows in the western direction through the Assam valley receiving other important tributaries like the Subansiri, the Manas, the Sankosh and the Tirtha from the north, the Buridihing, the Disang, the Dikhon, the Dhansiri, the Kopili from the south. The Brahmaputra traverses the Assam valley for 450 miles and its channel oscillating from side to side over a bed of six miles wide. The Barak, after traversing for a distance of about 60 miles from Tipaimukh, debouches into plains at Lakhipur where it turns west in the plains district of Cachar through which it flows. No body can deny the fact that one of the major problems of the North-East is the recurring floods in the Brahmaputra Valley and Barak Valley. The damage caused by floods and erosion of land annually in average is about Rs. 10 crore and on an average about 8,000 hectares area affected annually.

Pisciculture: Fish farming requires special attention for rural upliftment. Due to floods and high rainfall, an extensive cultivable water area is left unexploited every year. Lakes are ideal for fish farming in this region. The total cultivable water area available for fish farming is much high in Assam. There is a gradual decline of the indegenous fish population due to change in the ecology of this region. This led to price hike.

Sericulture: Another aspect of rural uplift in the North-East is sericulture. Though it is unknown as to when silk industry was introduced in India, some authorities claim that it was first introduced in Assam. The ancient kings of Assam took personal interest for the growth of sericulture. Because of the patronage, there was an advancement; it was obligatory for every village house to weave silk fabric. In the North-East, women were famous for weaving. But with the process of modernization, this household industry, which is an important aspect of rural uplift, especially of women is on the decline. With the help of modern technique, without destroying the culture, a lot can be contributed to the growth of this domesticated industry.

Handicrafts: The whole of the North-East region is well-known for the useful and fashionable articles made out of cane, wood and bamboo. Chairs, tables and various other kinds of furniture are made out of cane. It is also a raw material for paper industry in Assam. Similarly, the shortfall in the supply of sugar-cane is leading to low production in the sugar mills in the State.

Shortage of Technical Manpower

The land reform policy to be effective in North-East India should not be divorced from land utilisation policy. This pan of the policy requires technical manpower. In this region, the major constraint in rural uplift is the extreme inadequacy of trained manpower. Since Independence, this deficiency has been realised not only by the people of this region but also by the governments and different bodies like the North-Eastern Council, deeply involved in the development of this region. The North-Eastern Council since its inception has been seized of the problem of trained manpower—technical and non-technical—in the region. A series of discussions and studies were also undertaken under the auspices of the Council. But no effective measures have been taken to solve it. Schools, colleges and universities are coming up for imparting general education. Even in rural areas, general education institutions have been established in large numbers. But sufficient educational institutions on the vocational line to develop trained manpower are still not coming up. The schools and colleges, particularly in the rural areas are not having adequate facilities or infrastructure to render the service effectively. The most pertinent point is the lack of supervision over these basic institutions by the government or the authorities concerned. This has to be looked into immediately.

PRIs and People's Participation

Mention may be made of the late Rajiv Gandhi's efforts for rural uplift through the Panchayati Raj system as envisaged in the Constitution (73rd Amendment) Act, 1992. The Panchayat institutions may be involved in the planning, formulation and implementation processes. The members of the Panchayat with the help of voluntary organisations may mobilise and organise the villagers to demand for quality service and it may also generate community-based accountability on the performance of village level machineries for rural uplift. It will also help not merely to know as to how indigenous resources are being destroyed and wasted but also to explore ways for utilization of human resource, local knowledge and skill for rural uplift. Thus greater community participation in the State's administration can be generated. The scope of direct participation in administration will certainly minimise to a great extent the feeling of deprivation , exploitation, distrust among the rural people and will help the establishment of mutual trust and understanding between the government and the rural masses. The Panchayati Raj institution will be a village based controlling authority with the position of commanding loyalty of the villagers.

Women's Access to Land

In the traditional patriarchal family life, woman did not have independent access to land. One of the main reasons attributed for this was the division of work based on physical differences. This tradition is so deep-rooted that still it is practised even by the enlightened families. However, there is a practical difficulty in these rural societies that after marriage the girl goes away to her husband's home. So this practice may cause some administrative difficulties. This custom and women's independent access to land cannot go together.

Lastly, deep-rooted corruption is one of the serious problems affecting the process of rural uplift in the North-East. There are several instances of involvement of political leaders and administrators in rice scandal, land scandal, smuggling of forest resource, etc. which adversely affected the rural uplift programme in the region.

7

Land Reforms and Empowerment of Women

Land continues to be the primal asset in the Indian context where three quarters of its population depend on agriculture for their livelihood. Land is the most important capital of rural India. The central objective of land reforms is to make it available to as many actual cultivators as possible with the expectation that it would ultimately lead to relatively higher rate of agrarian growth with social justice. Hence, a study of land reforms and women's empowerment and what is required to modify them i.e. land reforms, becomes important.

After giving a brief introduction, the paper examines land reform in its historical perspective. An attempt here has also been made to describe the various land reform measures adopted in India since Independence. Finally, the paper deals with land reforms and women's empowerment and also provides some suggestions for empowering women.

Land Reforms Defined

Land reforms can be conceived both narrowly and broadly. The early literature on the subject defined land reform as an integrated programme of measures designed to eliminate obstacles to economic and social development arising out of defects in the agrarian structure. This broad definition was short lived and there seemed to have a slight shift towards a narrower concept of land reforms. According to the narrow concept, land reform was defined as changes in land tenure systems and the accompanying changes in other institutions that are necessary to achieve the objectives for which changes in land tenure are sought. Doreen Warriner defined land reform in terms of 'the redistribution of property of rights in land for the benefit of small farmers and agricultural labourers. In other words, land reform means: (i) redistribution of land in favour of the landless and small cultivators, and (ii) tenancy reform.

In simple terms, land reform means 'land to the tiller', i.e. conferment of occupancy rights to those who are actual tillers of the soil. To put it differently, this intends to make actual cultivators the owners of the land they cultivate.

Historical Background

The history of land reforms in India is more than 3,000 years old. During the ancient period, communal ownership of land was prevalent and the village communities owned the land collectively and they were collectively responsible for the payment of a share of produce. In other words, land did not belong to the king but to the community or persons who cultivated it. During the medieval period, the king had no proprietary rights in land beyond a definite share of its produce. The person who first cultivates wasteland becomes ipso facto the owner of the soil.

During the Mughal period, successive waves of conquest, assignments of revenue and extension of the farming system resulted in the creation of an aristocratic class superior to the village communities. The Mughal conquerors usually allowed the Raja or chief of a subjugated State either to become a tributary, retaining his possession and receiving the revenue as before or to assume the position of a superior collector of revenue, receiving it from the headmen and ma'cing himself responsible for it to the government.

The British introduced new forms of land tenure which, for the first time in the history of the country, created on a large-scale private property, and individual ownership rights in land. In order to bring about stability in agriculture, the British introduced land settlement in 1793. In Bengal and neighbouring areas, they created a class of landlords. This was ailed the Zamindari system. The Zamindars were declared to be the proprietors of land and right to ownership of land was, however, subject to regular payment of rent revenue to the government. Later, the British introduced a temporary Zamindari settlement to otter States under which the Zamindars were made owners of land but the revenue they had to pay was revised periodically.

Another land system, which was introduced in Bombay and Madras and subsequently extended to north-eastern and north-western India, was the Ryotwari settlement. Under this system, the cultivator was to be recognised as the owner of his plot of land subject to the payment of land revenue. The settlement under the Ryotwari system was not made permanent. It was revised periodically after 20 to 30 years when the revenue demand was usually raised.

A third type of land system known as Mahalwari system, was introduced in the Ganga valley, the North-West Provinces, parts of Central India, and the Punjab. Under this system, the revenue was to be made village by village or estate *(mahal)* by estate with landlords or heads of families who collectively claimed to be the landlords of the village or the estate. In Mahalwari areas also, the land revenue was periodically revised.

Thus the structure of agrarian society evolved under the British rule, created a socio-economic set-up in which parasitism flourished, land concentration in the hands of the rural rich continued to grow, and landlessness and land hunger of the peasants mounted at an ever-increasing pace. Another feature was that the cultivators were ground down by a colossal burden of indebtedness because of evictions and insecurity of tenancy and rack-renting.

Post-Independence Scenario

Land reforms have been on the national agenda of rural reconstruction for a long time, particularly since Independence. The major objectives of land reforms consist of reordering agrarian relations to achieve an egalitarian social structure; enlarging the land base of the rural poor; increasing agricultural productivity and production; and infusing equality in local institutions.

In the post-Independence period, the origin of land reforms can be traced to the Congress Agrarian Reform Committee constituted under the chairmanship of J.C. Kumarappa (1949).

The salient facets of land reforms policy adopted were: (a) abolition of intermediaries and bringing tenants in direct contact with the government; (b) tenancy reforms to provide security to actual cultivators of land against eviction; (c) redistribution of land by imposition of ceiling on agricultural holdings; (d) consolidation of holdings; and (e) updating of land records.

The approach of the Kumarappa Committee exercised a considerable influence on the evolution of the land reforms policy in later years.

Land Reforms and Five Year Plans

From the beginning of the Planning era, land reform was

recognised as: (i) a means to improve agricultural producavity; and (ii) a tool to broaden the distribution of its ben-i efits among a larger number of people in rural areas.

Land reforms have been a common feature in all the Five Year Plans. Moreover, all the Plans aimed at abolition of the intermediaries and reformation in the tenancy so as to reduce rent; to provide security of tenures to the tenants; confirmation of ownership rights and starting a redistributive process by imposition of ceiling; preparation and maintenance of land record and cadastral surveys.

Land reforms have been given a new impetus in the light of the objectives of the Eighth Plan. (The Eighth Plan focuses attention on agrarian relations. It proposes to initiate steps to review and reformulate the land legislation and ensure effective implementation.) The inclusion of land reform laws in the Ninth Schedule of the Constitution is a step in this direction.

Land Reform Measures

Since Independence, the government has been laying adequate stress on implementation of land reforms. The land reform measures aimed at removal of structural impediments to increasing productivity and to ensure a fair degree of equity in the distribution of land resources. In the implementation of some such measures, laws were enacted to regulate land rent and provide security of tenure to the tenants. However, the success of implementation of various land reform measures varied from State to State.

In the following paragraphs an attempt has been made to describe the various land reform measures adopted in India since Independence.

Abolition of Intermediaries

The first step towards restructuring the land reforms was in the shape of abolition of intermediary tenures like

Zamindari, jagirs, inams, etc between the government and the actual tiller of the land. Abolition of the Zamindari system involved removal of intermediaries, conferring permanent rights in land on the actual cultivators and standardisation of land rents.

No reliable and complete data regarding gains of abolition of intermediary tenures is available as yet; however the following had been the result: (a) Estimated 20 millior tenants came in direct relationship with the State; (b) Emer gence of a class of self-employed middle class farmers whc own and work on land primarily with their own famil; labour; (c) Extensive areas of wastelands, forests, cultivabli fallows and lands of various categories vested in the State (d) About six million hectares of vested land was distrib uted amongst the landless and land poor.

Tenancy Reforms

The second aspect of land reforms in India has been th introduction of tenancy reforms. Tenancy reforms wei enacted in all States except Nagaland, Meghalaya an Mizoram. They provide for conferment of ownersip on the tenants by the State, execution of ownership by tenants on payment of reasonable compensation, security of tenure and fixation of rents. However, the implementation of these laws has not been uniform.

Tenancy reforms have been most effectively implemented in the States of West Bengal, Kerala, Karnataka and Jammu and Kashmir. In West Bengal, 14 lakh share-croppers have been recorded under 'Operation Barga'. In Karnataka, three lakh tenants were settled on 11 lakh acres of land by special land tribunals, set up for this purpose. In Kerala, through the tenants association, applications of 24 lakh tenants for conferment of ownership were accepted. Among the States with moderate effectiveness are Maharashtra and Gujarat. The States where the tenants at will and share-croppers are worst placed include Bihar, Uttar Pradesh, Rajasthan, Haryana, Punjab and Orissa.

On the whole, the adoption of tenancy reform measures could not yield the results up to the expectation because of two main factors—structural forces and the existence of legal flaws in tenancy acts.

Land Ceiling

By ceiling on land holdings we mean the fixing of the maximum size of a holding that an individual cultivator or a cultivator family may possess. Beyond this maximum size all land belonging to the landlord is taken over by the government to be redistributed among the landless labourers.

Legislation for imposition of land ceiling and acquisition of the surplus land were enacted by most States in the 50s and 60s. However, many of these legislation suffered from infirmities and contained loopholes. It was only in July, 1972 that the national guidelines on land ceilings were evolved in a conference held by the Prime Minister and the States modified or enacted the ceiling laws accordingly.

In the States of Jammu & Kashmir, Himachal Pradesh, Assam and West Bengal, the percentage of surplus land acquired are 25.51 per cent, 19.86 per cent, 9.12 per cent and 9.03 per cent respectively. These States can be identified as 'highly effective' States in the implementation of land ceiling programmes. The States of Andhra Pradesh, Bihar, Kerala and Rajasthan can be placed under 'moderate effective' where the area declared surplus ranged from 1.51 per cent to 2.33 per cent of the net sown area. The States of Gujarat, Haryana, Karnataka, Madhya Pradesh, Orissa, Punjab, Tripura and Uttar Pradesh are 'least effective' in implementation of land ceiling programmes.

Consolidation of Holdings

By consolidation of holdings, we mean the pooling together of the scattered pieces of land belonging to a single landowner. Special legislation have been enacted in various States to promote consolidation of holdings. The consolidation of holdings scheme has made very good progress in States like Punjab, Haryana and Uttar Pradesh, facilitating agricultural growth. Orissa, Bihar and Himachal Pradesh have also taken up consolidation in a big way. An area of 684.72 lakh ha has so far been consolidated.

Land Records

Correct and up-to-date land records are an essential precondition for effective implementation of land reform measures, particularly for scrutiny of tenure for tenants and share-croppers and consolidation of holdings. Nineteen pilot projects for computerisation of land records were taken up, one in each major State. These are fully financed by the Central government at the rate of Rs. 25 lakh each. The project is nearing completion in Morena district of Madhya Pradesh and, Dungerpur in Rajasthan. The progress in other States need to be expedited.

Despite the achievements in the sphere of land reforms, a lot more still remains to be done. Land is still the single most important asset in India and as has been stated above, even the small farm can be a viable economic unit both in terms of employment and income for a family.

Land Reforms and Women's Empowerment

In most parts of the country, and particularly among marginal and landless agriculturists, earning a livelihood is still a family endeavour. Various studies conducted have clearly pointed out that there are a large number of women who primarily derive their livelihood from working, sometimes on a regular basis and often on a seasonal basis, or attached labourers. These women generally belong to illiterate SC, ST and backward classes.

The major agricultural operations in which women generally work are transplanting, harvesting, cutting twigs and clearing the fields. They collect cow-dung for fuel and manure. They cut grass and sell it as fodder. They travel long distances and cut or collect firewood and sell it or bring it home for use. They do these and many other 'income bringing' jobs in addition to the household chores. Women belonging to tenant and small land owning families also work on their own lands, both actively and in supervisory roles. They also have technical knowledge of cultivation and hire labourers and supervise their work.

In spite of doing all these work, many of these women are very often listed in the census under the category of 'non-workers'. Their work is not always counted and recorded. Gail Omvedt has emphasised that women's tasks though very crucial and involving skills which have been acquired over generations, are treated as less important and of lower worth. Gail Omvedt also questions the assumption that women cannot be trained for the more highly skilled jobs, which pay more. Modernisation and development thus further marginalise women and lead to large-scale displacement of women from agricultural employment.

The social disabilities of women cultivators, in the sense of inability to leave family responsibilities, further lead to occupational immobility increasing economic dependency. Thus, the exploitation of rural women, specially that of the agricultural labourers, is carried on at two levels: first as members belonging to antagonistic social relations and secondly, as members within a household, due to patriarchy.

In a study by Maria Mies, it was found that the women did not need conscientisation to make them aware of their exploitation. The involvement of social activists, the legislature, the administration and political parties and other NGOs in the implementation of land reforms has created a very powerful lobby which could bring about not only economic but also social reforms. As a result, women particularly of the agricultural labour classes got deeply involved with the mass movements to force proper implementation of land reform legislation.

In another study by Kathleen Gough, it was found that as a consequence of implementation of land reforms, the lives of women have changed. They were less subordinate to the landlord and more subordinate to the men of their own groups. They were also more economically valuable, helping with sowing, weeding and harvesting. A few of them also worked in the homes of the landlords.

While the women among the agricultural labourers tend to benefit from land reform legislation, they are not placed on equal footing with men in the sphere of social relations. This is more due to the impact of the dominance of patriarchal familial structure in the Indian society. Gough is of the view that though agricultural labour women constitute a substantial proportion of the membership of parties and mass movements, they are hardly associated in matters of decision-making.

Mencher and Saradamoni have also emphasised that while women were regularly paid less than men, they contributed a higher proportion of their earnings to the household than the men. The women also felt that their main responsibility was the care and feeding of their children. Among the agricultural labourers especially the Dalits, women's work was still valued and women's position remained higher among the tenants and middle peasants.

Thus, if land reforms are properly implemented, then it can have a positive bearing on the conditions of women, giving them increased economic independence and an opportunity to march towards greater equality in legal, political and social rights.

Suggestions

In the preceding paragraphs, we have discussed how

women's movement and role of NGOs and social activists have helped in getting the status of women involved in agricultural work improved. But unfortunately, the above-cited studies nowhere mention in regard to empowerment of women so far landed property is concerned. How one can think about women's empowerment without giving legal status to women in landed property?

Though the Hindu Code Act and Hindu Succession Act provide equal rights and share to the children, both male and female, in parental proper! yet, due to patriarchal pattern of our society how many female children have got their share without legal litigations; it is a big question to be answered by the policy-planners and the implementing agencies. Mere policy declarations and enacting various Acts by different States may not empower women to hold, acquire and dispose of parental property. It requires effective measures for implementation and basic social reforms. In this context, a few suggestions may be given. At the time of mutation, extreme care should be taken to enter the name of both the husband and wife in land records. Now, most States have adopted computerised system of land records. If effective measures are taken the task would automatically become easier.

At the present moment, if the head of the family under extreme economic pressure wants to dispose of landed property, he need not require the consent of his wife. He simply contacts the buyer of the land and disposes of the property. In majority of the cases the empirical findings suggest that the male member of the family disposes of the property against the wishes of his wife for his wasteful expenditure. As a result, in course of time the family becomes pauper and is forced to live pauperish life.

But if the land is in the name of both husband and wife, the male member of the family will be legally compelled not to dispose of the property if the wife is not willing. Similarly, in the case of 'Operation Barga' the record of sharecroppers in the name of both husband and wife be entered for better safety and more social and economic stability.

The government records also suggest that crores of acres of land have been acquired by the government under the agricultural Land Ceiling Act and such land is distributed among the landless agricultural labourers, ex-army men and destitutes. The guidelines of the Central government and State governments clearly mention that while assigning the surplus ceiling land to the beneficiaries, a joint patta should be issued in the name of both husband and wife. But empirical studies (Mishra, 1992) suggest that in clear violation of the guidelines the patta is issued in the name husband only. If this is the situation, how can we talk is empowerment of the women and land reforms?

The earlier studies suggest that women are more involved in agricultural work in comparison to their male counterparts but without any legal right and being dependent or the male member of the family. Is it empowerment of the women? In the final analysis it may be mentioned that if we are really interested in empowering women, it is a must that they should have legal rights over land and be treated equal to their male counterparts. This will not only improve their social and economic status but will also provide stability, viability and better life for the whole of the family.

Our suggestions may seem to be a day-dream at the present moment, but in the near future this is going to be realised. To make this point more explicit, it would be in the fitness of the things to mention about empowerment of women in Panchayati Raj by way of the Constitution (73rd Amendment) Act, 1992. When this provision was made there was apprehension in every quarter that this will not work as women still live under extreme conservatism and would hardly come out of purdah and actively participate in the functioning of PRIs. But the recent elections to PRIs suggest that women's representation in Panchayati Raj has exceeded the reservation limit as in Karnataka 43 per cent, Madhya. Pradesh 38 per cent, West Bengal 35 per cent, women are representing in elective capacity in the PRIs. As such, we are optimistic of the fact that if women are not empowered by way of land reforms right now, the women activists may start a movement for this purpose and ultimately will be forced to take strict measures to make women's empowerment a reality.

Bibliography

Dantwala, M.L., *Indian Agriculture, An Introduction to the Problem,* National Information and Publications, Bombay, 1949.

"Definition of Personal Cultivation", *Indian Journal of Agricultural Economics,* Vol. 12, No. 1, Jan.-March, 1957.

Gadgil, D.R., "Land Reform", Presidential address to the 15th Annual Conference of the Indian Society of Agricultural Economics, *Indian Journal of Agricultural Economics,* Jan-March, 1954.

Gough, K., *Rural Change in South East India, 1950 to 1980s,* Oxford University Press, New Delhi, 1989.

Govt. of India, *First Agricultural Labour Enquiry,* New Delhi, 1950-51.

Haque, T. and Sirohi, A.S., *Agrarian Reforms and Institutional Changes in India,* Concept Publishing Co., New Delhi, 1986.

ICSSR Working Group Report, *Alternatives in Agricultural Development,* 1980.

Jha, S.C., *A Critical Analysis of Indian Land Reform Studies,* Asia Studies Press, Bombay, 1971.

Jodhka, S., "Development or Debt", A Study on Credit Relations in Haryana", Unpublished Thesis, Punjab University, Chandigarh, 1991.

Joshi, P.C. and Dutta, R. (eds.) Land Reform and Agrarian Change in India and Pakistan since 1947, *Studies in Asian Social Development,* Tata McGraw Hill, New Delhi, 1971.

Joshi, P.C., *Land Reforms in India, Trends Perspectives,* Allied Publishers, Bombay, 1975.

Khusro, A.M., *The Economics of Land Reforms and Farm Size in India,* McMillan Co. Ltd., Delhi, 1973.

Lal, S.K., *Social Perspective of Land Reforms,* Agricole Publications, New Delhi.

Minhas, B.S., "Rural Poverty, Land Distribution and Development", *Indian Economic Review,* New Delhi, 1970.

Mukerji, K., *Land Reforms,* H. Chatterjee and Co. Ltd., Calcutta, 1952.

Sorokin, P.A., *Social and Cultural Mobility,* Illinois: A Free Press of Glencoe, 1959.

Radhakrishnan, P., *Peasant Struggles, Land Reforms and Social Change in Malabar, 1836-1982,* Sage Publishers, New Delhi, 1989.

Rastyannikov, V.G., "Agrarian Evolution in a Multifarm Structure Society", *Experience of India,* Routledge and Kegan Paul, London, 1981.

Saroha, A.S., "Surplus Land Acquisition and Social Mobility in Rural Haryana", Unpublished Thesis, Punjab University, Chandigarh, 1994.

Sharma, M.L. and Puniya, U.K., *Land reforms in India : Achievements, Problems and Prospects,* Ajanta Publishers, New Delhi, 1989.

World Bank Staff, "Rural PC verty in India", Working Paper No. 279, Nov., 1978.

Appu, P.S., "Land Reform is dead, Long Live Land Reforms", Vol. VIII, No. 20, *Economic and Political Weekly,* Bombay, May, 1973.

Bardhan, P.K., "On the incidence of rural poverty in India", Vol.VIII, No. 4,5,6, *Economic and Political Weekly,* Bombay, February, 1973.

Bergmann, T., *Agrarian Reforms in India,* Agricole Publications, New Delhi, 1984.

Beteille, A., *Studies in Agrarian Social Structure,* Oxford University Press, New Delhi, 1974.

-------, *Equality and Inequality; theory and practice,* Oxford University Press, New Delhi, 1983.

Bhalla, G.S., *Changing Agrarian Structure in India, a Study of impact of Green Revolution in Haryana,* Meenakshi Prakashan, Meerut, 1974.

Chadha, G.K., *State and Rural Economic Transformation, the Case of Punjab (1950-85),* Sage Publications, New Delhi.

Dandekar and Rath, "Poverty in India"-II, 6 (1 and 2) *Economic and Political Weekly,* Bombay, 1971.

United Nations, Progress in Lund Reform, Third Report, New York, 1962, p.vi.

United Nations, Progress in Land Reform, Fourth Report, New York 1966, pp. 2-3.

Warriner Doreen, *Land Reform in Principles and Practice,* Clarendon Press, Oxford, 1969, p. xiv.

Lahiri, T.B., "Problem of Sustaining Gains Derived from Land Reforms," *Yojana,* Vol. 37, No. 8, May 15, 1993, p. 8.

Maheshwari, N.D, "Land Reforms in India", *Yojana,* Vol. 31, No. 22, December 1-15, 1987, p.4.

Government of India, Eighth Five Year Plan, 1992-97, Vol. II, Planning Commission, New Delhi, p. 40.

Nayyar, Rohini, "Land Reforms: Still A Relevant Issue", *Yojana,* Vol. 37, Nos. 14 & 15, August 15, 1993, p. 55.

Gopal Iyer, K., "Interface of Political and Administrative Will in the Implementation of Land Reforms in India", *The Administrator,* Vol. XXXVI, No. 2, April-June, 1991, p. 139.

Kar, Sitanshu Ranjan, "Agrarian Policies and Their Impact", *Teaching Politics,* Vol. VIII, Nos. 1-2, pp. 19-20.

Gopal Iyer, K., *op.cit.,* p. 139.

Sisodia, O.P., "Land Reforms for Social Change", *Kurukshetra,* Vol. XXXVIH, No. 3, December 1989, p. 19.

Eighth Five Year Plan, *op.cit.,* p. 34.

Omvedt, Gail, *We Will Smash This Prison! Indian Women in Struggle,* Orient Longman, Delhi, 1979.

Mies, Maria, et al., *Women-The Last Colony,* Kali for Women, Delhi, 1988.

Gough, Kathleen, *Rural Society in Southeast India,* Cambridge University Press, Cambridge, 1981.

Mencher, Joan P., *Agriculture and Social Structure in Tamil Nadu,* Allied Publishers, Delhi, 1978.

Saradamoni, K., *Filling the Rice Bowl,* Sangam Books. Hyderabad, 1991.

Mishra, S.N., *Land Reforms and Distributive Justice,* Mittal Publications, New Delhi.